# Sugar Art

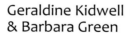

Geraldine Kidwell
& Barbara Green

Schiffer
Publishing Ltd

4880 Lower Valley Road · Atglen, Pennsylvania 19310

Schiffer Books are available at special discounts for bulk purchases for sales promotions or premiums. Special editions, including personalized covers, corporate imprints, and excerpts can be created in large quantities for special needs. For more information contact the publisher:

Published by Schiffer Publishing Ltd.
4880 Lower Valley Road
Atglen, PA 19310
Phone: (610) 593-1777; Fax: (610) 593-2002
E-mail: Info@schifferbooks.com

For the largest selection of fine reference books on this and related subjects,
please visit our web site at www.schifferbooks.com
We are always looking for people to write books on new and related subjects. If
you have an idea for a book please contact us at the above address.

This book may be purchased from the publisher.
Include $5.00 for shipping.
Please try your bookstore first.
You may write for a free catalog.

In Europe, Schiffer books are distributed by
Bushwood Books
6 Marksbury Ave.
Kew Gardens
Surrey TW9 4JF England
Phone: 44 (0) 20 8392 8585; Fax: 44 (0) 20 8392 9876
E-mail: info@bushwoodbooks.co.uk
Website: www.bushwoodbooks.co.uk

Designed by RoS
Type set in Bickley Script/Candara
ISBN: 978-0-7643-3382-8

Printed in China

# Sugar Art

Geraldine Randlesome
Barbara Green

Schiffer

# Dedication

To our husbands

# Acknowledgments

We send thanks to the many teachers who have so generously shared their talents: Nicholas Lodge, Charles Beasley, Roland Winbeckler, Brenda Harrington, Angela Priddy, Marithe de Alvarado, and many more. Thanks, too, for friends Leigh Sipe, Darlene Nold, Jean Beasley, Rosemary Watson, Frances Kuyper, Carol Webb, Vickie Anderson, Kathy Scott, Virginia Daniel ,and Jennifer Shearer for their help as well as their friendship.
—Barbara & Geraldine

I send many thanks and much love to my husband Bill. There are not enough words to show how much support and encouragement he has given me over the years. For years he gave me his Saturdays off to help with the delivery of many wedding cakes. He kept his cool when I was stressing out during deliveries and never complained about the many brides and their families that came to our home for interviews. Without his help and support I would not have been able to build my business, which has lasted over thirty years. I will be forever grateful. In addition I thank my children, Diane, Amy, and Jim, and my grandchildren, Jacob and Clay Martin, Lance Johnson, and great grandchildren Alyssa and Ava Martin for letting me practice my art on their birthday and special occasion cakes.

My mother Lillian T. Trapp spent her life teaching children. In retirement she started taking painting classes at the University of Kentucky. We, as well as our children, have many of her lovely paintings in our homes. She always encouraged me to express myself in art. However, my art took a different turn from hers as this book will show. I can only hope that my teaching of sugar art will inspire as many minds as she did over her years as a teacher. While going through my mother's belongings I found one of the first panorama eggs that I had made with royal icing stars for flowers and paper cut out for the scenes. She had kept and appreciated it for many years.

A special thanks to Brenda Harrington for introducing me to the wonderful world of gum paste and for the many ideas shared when we worked together to create beautiful eggs. Also, thanks to my friend Winnie from church for introducing me to sugar eggs. I never dreamed that a small act of friendship, sharing a craft, would lead to a career in cake decorating. I encourage you to enjoy the art, share you talent, and inspire someone.
—Barbara

I too would like to thank my husband Bill who is my childhood sweetheart, best friend, and right hand. Not only does he make special frames for me, he supports, transports, and donates every Saturday to helping me with deliveries. Thanks for the understanding of my children, Bret, Gina, and Lori and the support of my mother, Gladys. I only hope that my grandchildren, Bretani Munier Wiseman and Collan, Hunter, and Wesley Henderson can see that the hard work and dedication that I have put into my sugar art has produced a gratifying and successful business and will inspire them to know that any goal is within reach with perseverance.

A special thanks and note of support for the International Cake Exploration Societé, www.ices.org. This organization for sugar artists has given me the opportunity for continuing education, new products, travel, teaching, judging, and worldwide friends. Thanks I.C.E.S.
—Geraldine

# Contents

# Introduction

This informative book represents the collaboration of two Kentucky cake artists. Barbara Green and Geraldine Kidwell have been friends for many years, joined through the wonderful world of sugar art and cake decorating. For the first time, they have merged their talents and share numerous secrets with other decorators. It was an intriguing moment when they decided to join forces to construct a book on sugar molding and panorama eggs.

Barbara is extraordinarily talented in panorama eggs and sugar molding and has a wealth of knowledge as well as a collection of molds that she has gathered over the years.

Geraldine's decorating interests have ventured in other areas and she does not feel that her expertise in this area is as developed as Barbara's. It was, in fact, a huge pastillage panorama egg that first drew her inquisitive talents to the sugar world. Many years ago Geraldine was at a cake show in Louisville, Kentucky, where one of the entries was a large egg with a scene inside depicting a gum paste family going to church on Sunday morning. It was perfect in every detail. She thought it was the most spectacular display she had ever seen and that it could not possibly be sugar.

Because panorama eggs of different sizes lit the flame of thirst for knowledge in both Barbara and Geraldine, they hope this book will light the same fire within you.

Panorama Egg

The art of decorative eggs has been popular for many centuries. It is a popular item to decorate because of the attractive, smooth, oval shape of the egg. Large eggs such as duck or goose are normally blown through a small hole in one end to remove the contents. The emu egg is so large and strong that the shells can be carved without breaking.

Decorated eggs take many forms. Some are jeweled, like the famous jeweled Fabergé eggs, some carved, and other, more popular, eggs are dyed. Chocolatiers create works of art in chocolate eggs with cream centers.

Sugar molded eggs, called panorama eggs, reveal interior scenes of bunnies and chicks that have delighted children for many years. They can be used for table decorations and Easter baskets, or even suspended from flowering branches. Eggs are decorated by many cultures and exchanged as gifts. They are often referred to as a symbol of rebirth.

Do you think you are too old for an egg hunt? Well, whether you are interested in these panorama eggs or not, the sugar art concepts in this book will expand your vision of molded sugar into additional areas. Colored sugar can be molded into sugar roses and leaves for a special tea. Sugar boxes or tiny animals can be molded from sugar. The list could go on and limited only by imagination. We have carried the molding of sugar into various sugar mediums, using fondant, pastillage, and gum paste to decorate additional holiday cakes with molded items for your enjoyment with directions that allow you to recreate designs for every season of the year.

Sugar Art

*Basics*

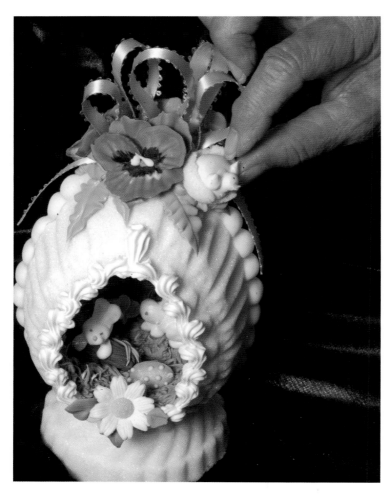

Panorama egg trimmed with ribbons and sugar flowers

## Supplies for Sugar Eggs

**Egg-shaped candy mold**
**Water**
**Granulated sugar**
**Paper towels**
**Royal Icing**
**Food colors**
**Pastry bags and decorating tips**
**Bowls**
**Sugar flowers**
**Sugar candy animals**
**Satin ribbon**
**Paper plate**
**Pencil**
**Sponge**

Sugar with lumps may need to be shaken through a sieve

## Preparing the Sugar

Super fine sugar is best for molding but can be very expensive. With a food processor, you can achieve the same super fine sugar using standard granulated or even hardened sugar that you have saved from a previous project. If you are working with hard, previously used sugar, you may need to sift the sugar through a strainer or sieve to remove any lumps. Place the sugar in the food processor and pulse for several minutes.

When the sugar is ground super fine, water can be added to it with the processor running to bring it to the consistency for molding. The ratio should be 1-1/2 teaspoons of water to 1 cup of sugar, which is 7-1/2 teaspoons of water to 5 cups of sugar. Stop and start the processor several times in pulsing action.

To make **colored sugar**, tint the water before adding it to the sugar and mix well. Failure to mix completely will result in spotting on the sugar. Colored sugar will fade over time so basic white sugar is recommended for the shells.

If the sugar and water are not mixed thoroughly, it can cause either wet or dry spots on the finished eggs. Dry spots will cause holes to form when you scrape out the egg. Wet spots will always look discolored. Place the sugar in a large bowl and mix well with your hands.

The sugar will dry out very quickly, so always keep it covered with a damp towel. Allow the sugar to rest for at least one hour before shaping.

Pour water slowly into sugar and pulsate

Pulsating sugar in food processor

Sugar pieces inside a food processor

Work sugar mixture with your hands

## Egg Molding & Decorations

Many years ago there were many molds being manufactured especially for sugar. Molds used in this book range from actual candy molds to plastic containers for candy and gifts that were found at drug and discount stores. Simply put, if a container is wider at the open end and has no undercuts you can use it to mold sugar. Tart pans work well for the bases of sugar eggs. Glass does not work as well as other mediums for sugar molding. Plastic Easter eggs are readily available before the holiday and come in various sizes.

The small molds are more difficult to find. Yard sales, flea markets and thrift stores are great places to explore for egg shapes. You can use a gum paste flower mold, a ball candy mold, or even a gum paste flower former that is a circular bowl shape. The egg-shaped plastic containers that hold small toys sold in vending machines are great for molding egg shells.

Some of the eggs come apart lengthwise. These are used for the panorama eggs as they have additional height for the scene. Chocolate candy molds work well and are available through cake and candy retail supply stores. Remember, the larger the mold the harder it is to turn the molding out. Egg cake pans and oval plastic dishes make good alternative molds for larger eggs.

Clear plastic molds

Various plastic molds

Easter candy molds

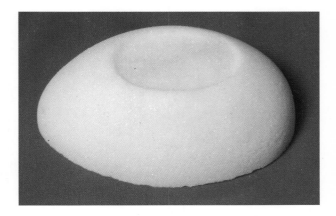

Pack the sugar and water mixture into half of an egg mold. Wipe away any mixture that extends beyond the mold. Place the mold with the sugar mixture onto the traced shape of the egg mold. Lift the mold, leaving the molded sugar on the tray.

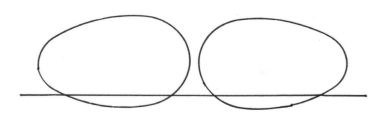

For a side opening, make a pattern with the two halves laid end to end. Mark the opening cut 1/2 inch from the long side.

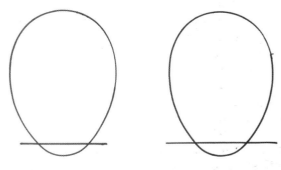

For a front opening, lay the egg patterns side-by-side and mark the cut 1/2" from narrow end.

The opening for the top and bottom of the eggs needs to be cut exactly the same to insure a consistent opening size. It is best to draw a pattern of each half on a piece of cardboard or parchment. Tape the pattern to a cookie sheet to prevent it from slipping. For eggs that open on the side, place the ends of the eggs molds together back to back and draw a line 1/2-inch from one long edge. For an egg that has the opening in the end, mark and cut across the tip of the egg using a heavy thread or dental floss. Hold the thread taut and slice through the damp sugar. Place the excess sugar back in the bowl and keep covered with a moist towel. Be sure to cover the cut edge of the egg with layers of damp paper towels to prevent it from drying.

Turn the sugar egg onto pre-marked pattern and cut with heavy thread or dental floss held taut.

End opening removed from top shell

Cut several layers of paper towel and moisten. Place them over the cut area of the sugar egg to keep it moist. An alternative would be to place a piece of plastic wrap over the flat bottom and an oval cookie cutter on top to hold it in place. Either method will retard the drying of the opening and allow more even drying of the whole egg.

Let the outer part of the egg dry and harden. Drying time will depend upon the temperature and humidity of the room. When the outer part of the egg has dried 1/4 inch deep, use a spoon to scoop the wet sugar from the center. Leave more sugar in the bottom of standing eggs so the designs are at the level of the opening. Sugar is cheaper than royal icing.

Before adding decorative elements to the inside the egg, be sure to dust out all of the loose sugar from each half.

The interior of the egg can be decorated in a number of ways. We prefer that everything be edible, but many eggs are decorated using purchased candies and novelties. Bunnies, chicks, and flowers used in this egg are described in detail in another part of this book.

A bunny for this egg was molded in a candy mold with fondant and colored with powdered colors and food safe pens.

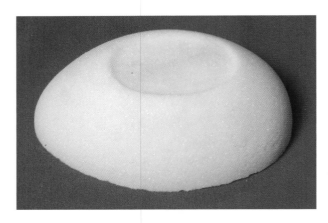

The flat bottom of this candy egg mold will be cut away to make the front opening of a stand-up egg.

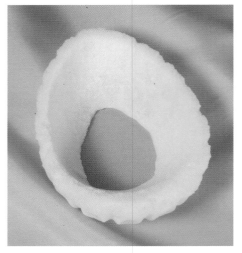

Front half with opening removed

Add royal icing greenery to the lower grass area of the inside of the hollowed out sugar egg. For additional grass a #233 grass tip can be used.

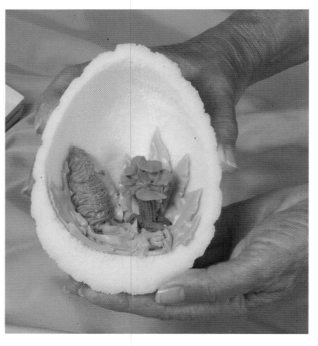

Arrange royal icing trees in the back half of the egg.

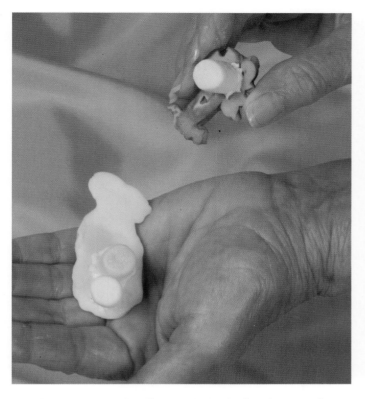

Attach miniature marshmallows to the back of the bunny with royal icing to add stability to the figure.

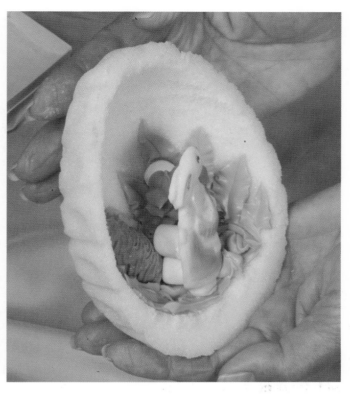

Add additional royal icing and position the bunny into the back half of the egg.

Place bunny into egg. Add royal icing grass and flowers to the front half of the egg.

Both halves of the egg are decorated, which gives it three-dimensional depth when viewed from the front.

When the decorations are finished, plastic containers can be used to hold the egg segments while they dry. Position them so that the figures are straight up.

Set back of the egg into container to dry in upright position

The front of the egg, seen from the back.

Remove the dried eggs from the container and line up the two pieces.

Apply a line of royal icing to the edge of the front half of the egg, using a small star tip #14 or #6 round tip. Apply enough to glue the back portion to the front without any overflow of frosting.

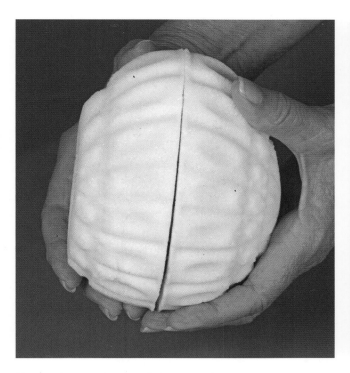

Line up the two pieces and place together.

Use your finger to remove any excess royal icing from the seam and smooth.

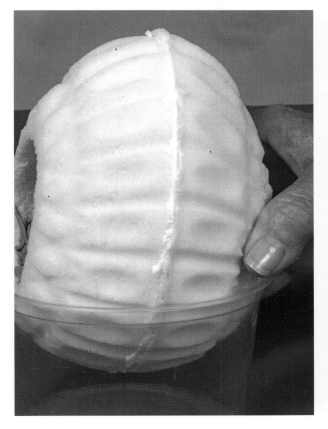

Place the combined halves in an appropriate container to support it in an upright position...

...until the royal icing dries and secures the bond between the two halves.

Apply a dab of royal icing to a pre-molded, appropriate size sugar base as pictured.

Position the egg into the royal icing. Press egg onto base to secure, supporting it, if necessary, and allow the ensemble to dry.

A thin rope of fondant, shaped in a pearl maker mold, will conceal the seam. Moisten the back of the pearl rope with water and position it over the seam of the egg.

One alternative decoration is to pipe a royal shell border over the seam. Another way of concealing the seam is to cover it with the same satin ribbon that was used for the ribbon loops, adding a small shell border of royal on each side of the ribbon.

Roll a fondant rope.

Press the rope into a pearl maker mold, making sure to trim the excess from the edges of the mold.

Apply the pearled strip to the seam of the egg.

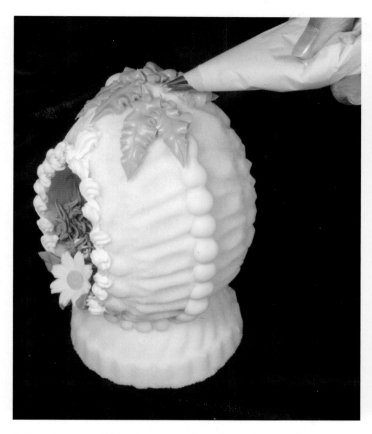

Pull out long, royal icing leaves as a foundation for your decorations...

...and build up in the center top as a base to secure ribbon loops.

Add loops of ribbon using a skewer to press the loops into the icing to secure. If you are making a large number of eggs, do not cut the lengths of ribbon. Instead, cut the ribbon when all of the loops and tails are pressed into the icing. This will prevent the waste of excess cut ribbon. It will take approximately 1/2 to 3/4 yard of ribbon, depending on the size of the egg. Loops should be 1-1/2 to 2 inches high. Leave a 2 inch tail on each side of the egg.

### Before the royal icing dries, add the flowers.

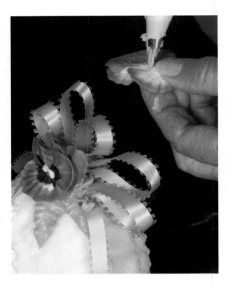

Pipe green royal icing to the back side of the royal icing flowers...

...and press into the wet royal icing leaves.

Place small amounts of royal icing between the loops of ribbon.

*Important Hints for Molded Sugar*

1- To color sugar, add the food color to the water before adding the water to the sugar. Mix the sugar and colored water well to get an even distribution of color.

2- When coloring small amounts of sugar, place the sugar, water, and food color in a zip lock bag to mix.

3- In warm climates, store sugar eggs with moth balls to keep insects away. Note that eggs are for decoration and not to be eaten.

4- Do not eat, drop, or get eggs wet. They will last for many years if stored properly.

5- Do not use the same mold for sugar and chocolate. The sugar will scratch the molds.

6- Save a few broken egg shells to practice different methods of coloring the animals. You can use powdered food colors to brush color on the animals. Simple syrup mixed with food color will bleed if the syrup is too thin. The sugar works like a sponge. It is best to try a sample first and not ruin a finished animal.

7- Some polymer clay techniques can be used for fondant and gum paste.

8- There may be slight color variations between different brands of sugar. If you are doing a large number of eggs, it is advisable to stay with one brand.

## Molding Sugar Animals

Sugar bunnies and chick

Sugar bunny and lambs

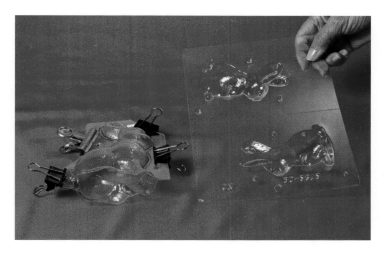

Cut mold with enough of an edge that the sides can be clipped

Tiny sugar molded items can be used inside the panorama eggs. Larger molds, such as chocolate molds, can be used for free standing displays.

Plastic, 3-D candy molds work very well when making dimensional sugar animals. Some molds are closed at the bottom and some are open. The molds that are open at the base are much more difficult to use for sugar molding.

With the mold open, pack the damp sugar firmly into both halves of the mold, leaving a little excess sugar in the mold. Line the two pieces together and clip the edges together. Turn the mold upside down and pack more sugar into the bottom and press hard. Lay the mold down and unclip. Gently remove the top of the mold. Let it dry 2 hours, then turn the figure over and remove the other half of the mold. Continue to dry.

For molds that are closed at the bottom, pack both sides with damp sugar. Leave some excess sugar on each half. You need the excess sugar because of spillage that happens when placing the pieces together.

Pack sugar firmly into bunny halves

Hold one half in each hand and slap the two halves together being sure to align the edges.

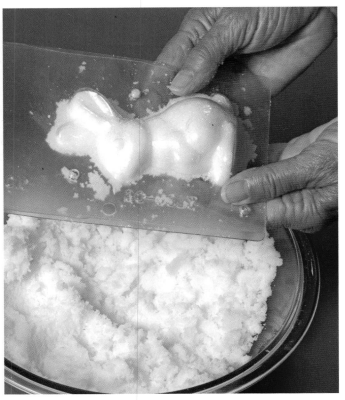

Use your fingers to firmly press the two molded halves together, carefully aligning the edges.

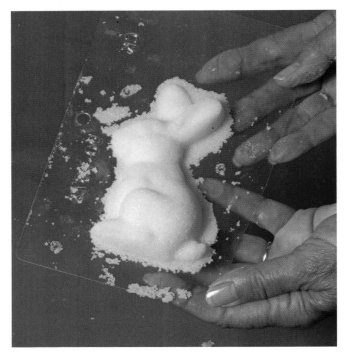

Very carefully, remove the top half of the mold. Allow the figure to dry 3 to 4 hours before turning it over and removing the other half of the mold. Do not touch the figure while the sugar is drying.

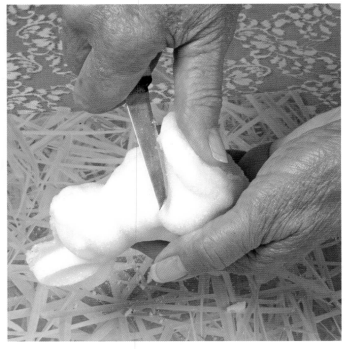

When the figure is completely dry, use a small paring knife to carefully scrape the excess sugar from the animal's seams.

Brush powdered colors on the figure, using a small paint brush to color the ears and cheeks.

A simple syrup and food coloring can also be used. To cook simple syrup, boil equal parts of water and sugar for 3 minutes and let it cool. Use an artist pallet to mix the simple syrup with food color. Sugar will work like a sponge, so always test the simple syrup "paint" on a scrap of sugar. It is best to try a sample rather than to ruin a good decoration. If the sugar syrup bleeds, you should cook it a little longer. If it is too thick, dilute it with a few drops of water. Save a few broken sugar egg shells to practice on.

For detail marking you can use a food safe pen.

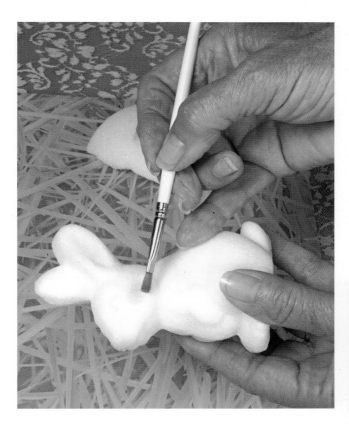

Paint cheeks and ears

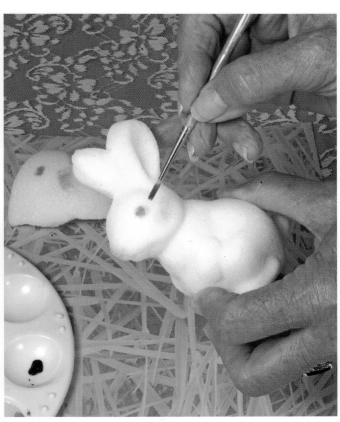

Paint the eyes

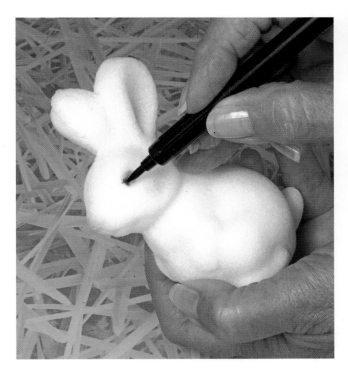

Add the pupil in eye with a food safe pen

## Large 3-D Bunny

There is a large range of mold sizes, ranging up to this one that is over 1 foot tall. It produced a beautiful, detailed bunny.

The egg in the bunny's paws is painted with thick simple syrup tinted with food coloring. The bow is satin ribbon. The basket was painted with simple syrup colored brown. The grass is piped with tip #233 and royal icing. Royal icing drop flowers and fondant molded eggs accent the completed design.

Large bunny mold

Large bunny with basket

Three sizes of molded bunnies

## Flat Bunny

This bunny is molded with fondant in half of a 3-D mold. First dust the mold liberally with corn starch. Press the fondant into the mold, leveling the back side with your hand. Leave a little extra fondant at the base of the bunny to help in removing it from the mold. This will also help the bunny stand. Turn the bunny out to dry. It can be colored with dusting powder, food pen, or food coloring that has been diluted with alcohol.

One-sided molded bunny

Molded chick and baby bunny

## 3-D Chick and Bunny

The 3-D chick and bunny are molded in the same way. After drying, sand the base on a sanding board before attaching it to a molded base with royal icing. Tart pans or candy molds can be used as bases.

Color the features; add a satin bow, green royal icing, drop flowers, and a sugar lay-on egg have been used to finish the designs. Note: for the small sugar eggs, sanding each half on a sanding board will produce a better joint.

**3-D Lamb**

As with all 3-D molds, trace around the outside of the lamb with a black permanent marker. Cut the mold apart with scissors to be able to mold each piece separately. The base for the lamb is molded in a candy plaque mold.

Decorate the lamb with royal icing grass, fondant flowers and purchased royal icing eggs. The lamb's face is painted with diluted simple syrup tinted black. The features, ears and tail were painted with simple syrup colored with food coloring. You should always try your simple syrup on a scrap of molded sugar before attempting to use it on the finished piece. Use a small amount of royal icing to add a satin ribbon around the edge of the plaque.

The molded and decorated lamb

Lamb mold outlined with permanent marker

Molded base for lamb

## Rabbits from Antique Molds

These sugar rabbits are molded in antique cake/gelatin molds. Pack the rabbit mold solidly with sugar. The small rabbit does not have to be scooped out. Due to the weight of the large rabbit, however, it is advisable to remove some sugar after the outside shell has dried to 1/2 to 3/4 inch thick. Antique shops, flea markets and yard sales are good locations to search for this type mold. The rabbit would be adorable to use on the side of a basket weave Easter cake.

Antique rabbit molds

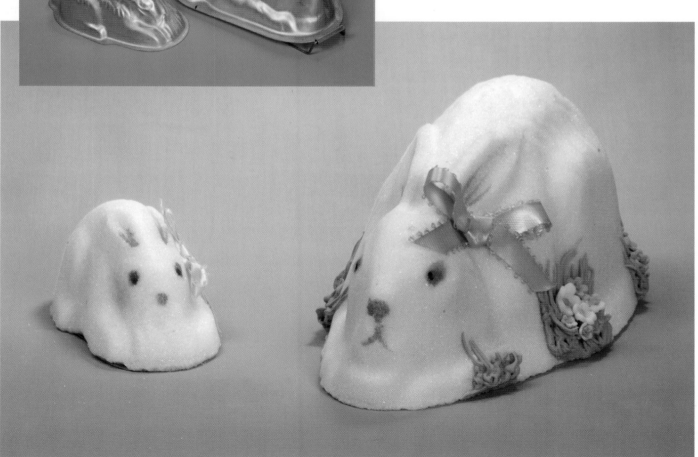

Rabbits molded in antique molds

## Baby Chick in an Egg

Tiny plastic egg molds are very difficult to find even around the Easter holiday. As a replacement for these molds you can use a 1 inch candy bon-bon mold like the ones that are shaped for chocolate covered cherries.

Pack moist sugar into the candy mold and allow it to dry for a couple of hours, depending on the temperature of the room. Make extra shells as there will be breakage. The shell should be very thin. When you are scraping out the soft sugar, chip the edges to resemble a cracked egg shell. The little chick is piped directly into the little shell. Use food safe pens to color the eyes and beak.

Baby chick in sugar shell

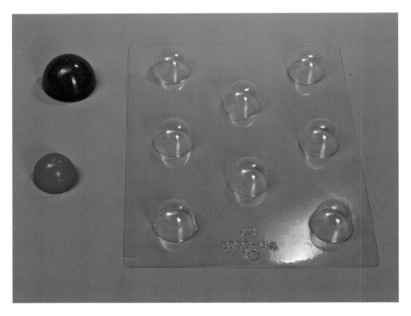

Bon-bon molds for sugar shell

Scraping out tiny sugar shell

## Closed Hollow Eggs

Sugar eggs do not need to be open, but they should be hollowed out. Leave the base thicker than the top for stability. If two eggs are going to be used together, as shown here, the eggs need to be facing each other during decoration. Apply ribbons horizontally in opposite directions attaching them with small dots of royal icing.

You can pipe royal icing bunny figures with a tip #6. Add royal icing grass with a tip #3 and royal borders with a tip #16 or #18. Tie and attach petite bows to the top of the egg with a small dot of colored icing the same color as the bow. When the royal icing bunnies have dried, add facial features with a food safe pen.

Molded eggs with opening

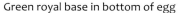

Green royal base in bottom of egg

Arrangement of candies in base of egg

## On the Half Shell

The scene inside an egg can also be created on one half of the shell with the other half creating a dome over the scene.

Dust out any loose sugar and apply a base of green royal icing with a spatula to the inside base of the sugar egg. Icing applied directly to the sugar with a grass tip will not stick if you do not apply the base first. Add the sheaves of grass while the icing is moist, and insert pre-made royal icing trees, flowers, bunnies, and eggs.

You can vary the scenes by using duck or chicks in some and bunnies in others. For the baby ducks it is attractive to place a small amount of blue royal into the base for a pond for the little duck. Other scenes have royal bunnies peeping over logs or sugar lay on bunnies with royal icing carrots.

Top view of the duck on pond base

Duck on pond in base of egg, back view

Bunny scene in base of egg                                    Fox peeping over log

Horizontal scene egg on a base

## Horizontal Eggs

These eggs are designed to lay horizontally and are placed on sugar bases using royal icing. Royal icing stars are added to cover the seams.

Tiny ducks or bunnies grace the interior of the eggs and purchased royal icing flowers are applied to the top with royal icing leaves and royal drop flowers. The bunny was figure piped with royal icing. The eyes and nose are piped with a tip #1 and colored royal icing.

Duck inside egg

Bunny inside egg

The swans swim in the bottom half of the egg. Flowers and leaves decorate the assembled egg.

### Swans

The swans were molded in a plastic candy mold with fondant/gum paste. Royal icing leaves and flowers decorate the top. The interior has a lake scene to properly display the swans in their natural habitant.

A swan mold

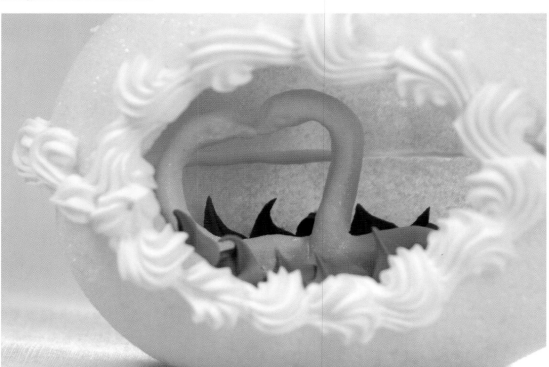

Close-up of swans inside the egg

## End & Side View Eggs

The egg with the pink flower is molded with light yellow colored sugar and has the opening for the scene at the tip of the egg. As described earlier, the end is removed from the damp molded sugar by pulling a taunt thread across the marked end and removing the excess sugar. Ribbon loops and shaded royal icing pansies adorn the top.

The second egg has a side opening. The top arrangement has purchased royal icing violets and a daisy molded from fondant in a silicone mold. They are attached to the egg with green royal icing leaves.

Other pictured eggs show variety in shape, opening and decorations so that each has its own individual personality.

End view egg

Side view egg decorated with molded daisy

Side view egg decorated with a rose

Decorated eggs

Decorated eggs and bunny

Decorated eggs and base mold

Molded bunny on top of egg

## Bunny-topped Egg

This bunny-topped sugar egg is sure to delight every youngster at Easter time. The bunny is hand molded of fondant.

Do not let the pieces dry completely, adding them to the egg while they are still pliable enough to conform to the shape of the top of the egg.

Mold the fondant pieces with a tear drop shape for the body and a smaller oval for the head. Form small ovals for both front and back feet, flattening one end of each piece. Use a knife to imprint toe marks. For the ears, mold two small long ovals and make impressions down the middle of each piece with a small paint brush handle.

Add royal icing grass to the top of the egg with tip #233.

Arrange the bunny feet in the wet grass.

Add the body over the legs. To form the eyes either paint them with a food pen or use tiny pieces of colored fondant balls. For the nose add a tiny pink fondant ball or pipe with a pink royal icing dot. Dust the inside of the ears with pink pearl luster dust.

## Working with Large Molds

The large sitting bunny is solid molded sugar and weighs 3 pounds or more when completed. The base is a plaque mold, but any shallow, rectangular box or pan could be used to mold the base. The grass is piped with a #233 grass tip with accents of royal icing flowers. It is recommended that heavy paper be secured to the bottom of the sugar base to prevent it from scratching furniture.

Large sugar bunny

*Molding Helps & Hints*

1- The larger the mold, the more difficult it is to pack. A piece of "egg crate" foam on a heavy metal tray will provide stability while the mold is being filled. Simply lay the mold on the foam rubber while packing it.

2- For extra support for weak spots, like the legs and ears, embed drinking straws into the sugar.

3- After joining the two halves of the bunny mold together, place it on the foam rubber. Use the palm of your hand to firmly press the two halves together. Gently remove the top half of the mold.

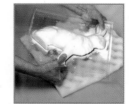

4- Allow bunny to dry on foam for support. For large pieces of molded sugar, leave it in the bottom mold for two days. When it is dry, place a piece of foam on the molded bunny and gently turn it over.

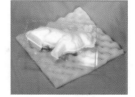

5- Remove the back portion of the mold. Leave the bunny on the foam for an additional two days to completely dry.

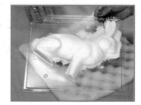

## Figure Piping

The basic shapes for figure piping are the ball, shell, and oval. By making them larger, smaller, fatter, or longer you can achieve many designs. In addition, by changing the size you can make many different animals.

Basic figure piping shapes

For a basic bunny, pipe the ears before the head is added to get a better connection. Pipe the bunny body as a large shell.

Steps to pipe a bunny and carrot. Pipe the carrot in advance so it can be added to a wet body. Add the ball head between the ears and body then pipe the hind legs and the arms.

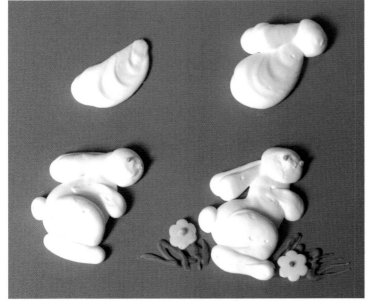

Piping a side view of a bunny

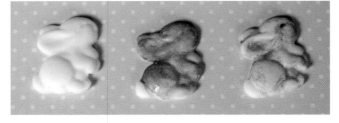

Coloring figure piping. Do not paint the bunny tail. Wipe off the excess color with a damp tissue as if you were antiquing furniture. White bunnies only need their facial features painted and, occasionally, the inside of their ears.

To color dry fondant animals for the inside of an egg use a darker shade of food color mixed with vodka.

## Trees

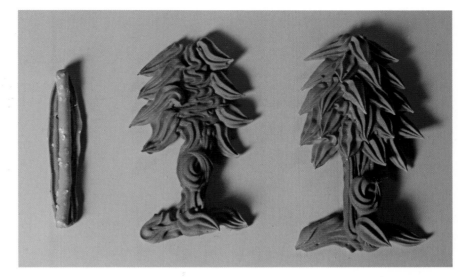

To make a piped pine tree with a trunk, pipe a line of brown royal icing on a tray lined with a piece of waxed paper. It is easier to move the tray than the paper alone. Add a stick pretzel for strength, and pipe the tree over the pretzel. Add the greenery with a #16 star tip.

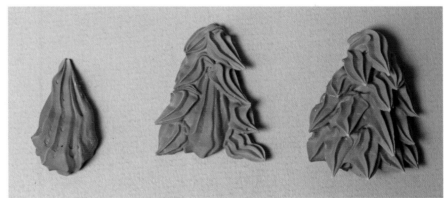

For a tree without the trunk, pipe a shell. Use the #16 star tip to pull out foliage.

To form a log, pipe a line of brown royal icing. Add the stick pretzel into the damp royal icing, then pipe additional frosting over the pretzel with a small star tip. This will form rough ridges in the log. Attach a sugar lay-on bunny head behind the log with some royal icing.

## Chicks, Ducks, & Birds

The little chick and duck are piped very similarly, but with a change to the length and shape of the beaks. Pipe the beaks with a deeper yellow or orange royal icing. Add the ball head then the shell-shaped body. Add a smaller shell for the wing. An eye completes the little chick. Pull the icing to a point for the duck's tail.

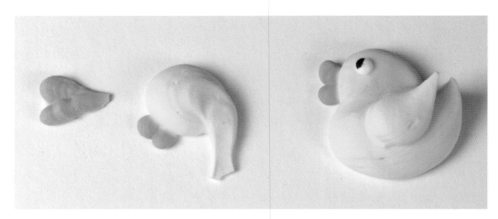

Pipe three long teardrops for the tail feathers. Two connected long ovals pulled to a point form the wings with an oval shape body connecting the tail and wings. Pipe a small ball for the head and add a tiny beak. The color of the bird can determine the type bird such as white for a dove, a blue bird, or red for a little cardinal. The dove works well for wedding cakes.

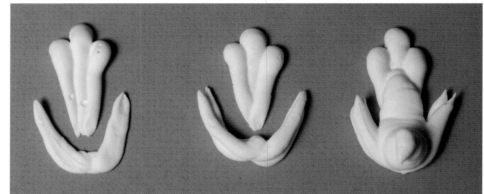

## Pansies

A pansy is so typical of spring that it is perfect for panoramic eggs. Place a square of waxed paper on a #7 flower nail. Use a tip #104 and start in the center of the square. Squeeze the bag as you move back with a slight jiggle. Turn the nail as you jiggle and return to the point where you started. Add two additional petals on the top of the two that you just piped. Add one larger petal to the base of the flower by turning the nail as you jiggle. When you actually attempt this you will see that it is easier than it sounds.

## Sugar Cubes

For that special occasion, when every tiny detail is crucial, make a spectacular impression with colorful molded sugar cubes for your tea or coffee. These tiny molded leaves and hearts add that extra special touch. This would be a perfect display for Mothers Day, a luncheon, shower or even a tea.

Molded sugar for tea or coffee

# Decorating
*through the*
# Seasons

# Spring

Spring is a time when the world becomes fresh and green. A time for flowers to bloom, birds to sing, and trees to bud. It is a time for baby bunnies to hop and chicks to hatch. It is a time for new beginnings so it might be the perfect time for you to begin a new hobby in sugar art.

## *Fabergé Type Box*

After you have practiced with all of the various shapes of sugar eggs, you may want to expand your knowledge and create something a little more elaborate and elegant. The Fabergé-style egg is very beautiful and can be used for a candy or jewelry box.

For a mold, use a large egg that opens like the one pictured. Large plastic eggs can be found before Easter as containers for candy or gifts, and make a good mold.

As you apply the sugar or fondant to the mold, make the bottom of the egg shell thicker than the top. If the bottom half is heavier it provides a better balance. A candy mold base works well to hold a stand-up egg. Allow all pieces to dry.

Note: A fondant egg takes longer to dry than sugar but it works much better for pearl dust.

Make a thin strip of fondant approximately 1/2 inch wide and place it in the upper edge of the egg bottom with 1/4 inch protruding above the shell edge as described for the heart box. Attach the strip with a damp brush or royal frosting. This will make a lip that keeps the top half of the egg from sliding off.

For lace accent pieces and borders, you can use fondant lace molds or polymer clay molds. The polymer clay molds are available in craft stores and the fondant molds available from cake supply shops.

To form the finial design on the top piece, roll a small ball and flatten. Roll another smaller ball, flatten and attach it to the first ball. Add other accent pieces while still damp and attach them with a little alcohol. Paint the entire trim pieces with a mixture of pearl luster dust and vodka or pure lemon flavoring.

Plastic molds

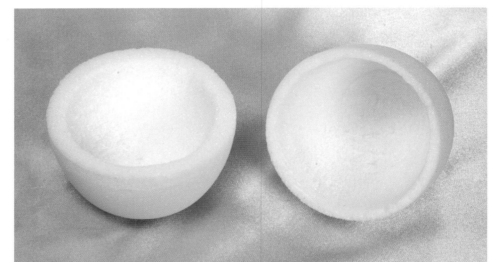

Molded egg

Polymer clay mold for the lace trim

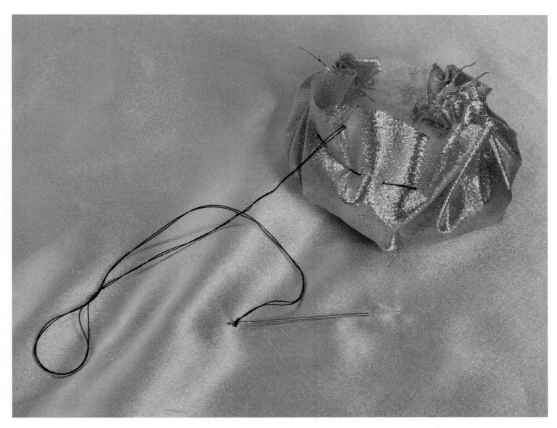

To create a cushion for the inside of the egg, use a needle and thread to gather a small circle of light weight fabric with a little fiberfill inside.

Place the gathered side down and place the cushion inside the bottom portion of the box, attaching it with royal icing. This forms a pretty base for jewelry or other gifts.

## *Medium Side-View Egg*

Mold the moist sugar in a medium size egg mold, as previously described. A tiny bunny family is gathering a basket of eggs in the scene of the egg. Form a base as described for other eggs and attach the egg to it with royal frosting.

Completed view of medium egg

Close-up view of scene

## The Lace Trim

A variety of lace pattern molds can be purchased through cake decorating shops or internet stores. Press fondant into a mold such as the one pictured. Gently loosen the lace from one end and gently remove from the mold. If you have difficulty removing the lace, place it into the freezer for a few minutes.

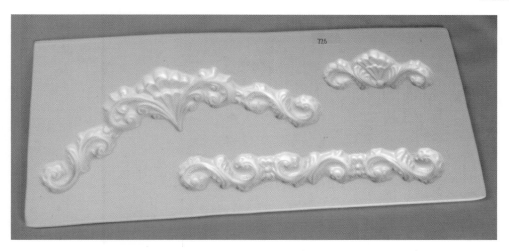

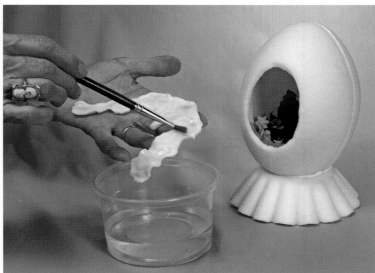

Lightly brush the back of the lace with a damp brush...

...and place around the opening of the egg.

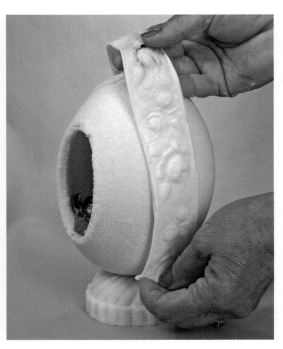

A long molded piece of rolled fondant covers the seam where the egg meets the base.

## Decorating the Top

Some eggs have a mound of royal icing on top of the egg to arrange flowers and others have a ball of fondant to form a mound on top of the egg that makes a base for the flowers.

Royal icing or fondant on top of the egg will secure ribbons to it

If you wish to elevate floral arrangement add a mound of fondant.

Add satin ribbon loops into the soft fondant.

Lovely sugar orchids have been purchased in white so they could be colored any color to match the theme. Assemble the gum paste orchid.

Brush the flower with the appropriate color dusting powder...

...and brush the leaves with green.

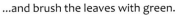

Arrange the flowers and leaves in the ribbons with royal icing.

### Royal Egg

This egg is so stately and elegant that it is lovely enough for royalty. It is very large and was molded in an egg shape cake pan. A large gelatin mold was used for the base. It is necessary to gently scoop out some of the sugar from the base to create a hollow area in which the egg can stand. The close-up view shows the tiny board fence and the royal painted bunny hopping along.

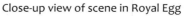

Close-up view of scene in Royal Egg

## Making the Rose

The top of the royal egg is built around a fondant rose.

Roll out a thin sheet of fondant mixed with Tylose powder and cut numerous rose petals with a gum paste flower cutter.

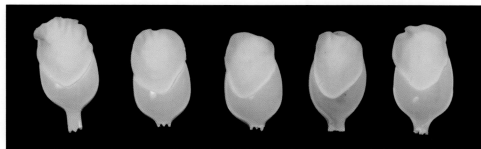

Arrange the petals in plastic spoons in a curved shape and let them dry just long enough to hold their shape.

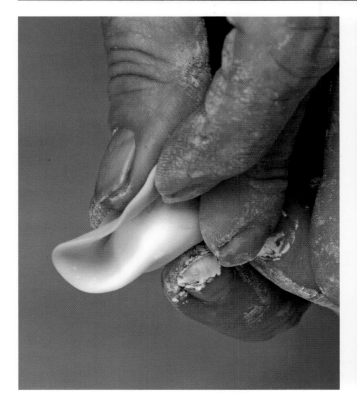

Roll one petal tightly for the center of the rose bud.

Continue adding petals, interleaving them until you get the size bud that you think would fit the top of the egg.

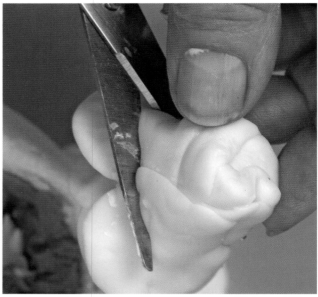

Use scissors or a knife to cut excess fondant from the back of the rose so that it will fit snugly on the egg.

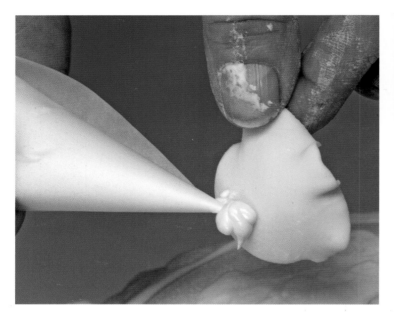

Use royal icing to attach rings of the petals around the top of the egg, starting at the outside and working layers of petals to the center top of the egg. When the petals are added in this manner directly to the top of the egg, they contour better to the curve.

Position three or four rows with royal icing and position the bud in the center of the rings of petals. Nestle fondant leaves under the outside edge of the rose for this result.

## Lace Appliqués

The sides of the royal egg are decorated with lace fondant appliqués.

Mold lace appliqués from fondant in a cake decorator's silicone mold. There are numerous designs available.

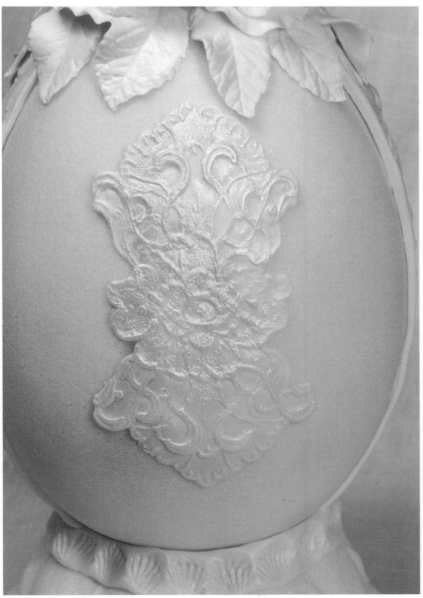

Fondant lace on egg

## *Sugar Heart Box & Cake*

Expand your vision of sugar molding and do not confine it to sugar eggs. This dainty two-piece heart can be used for jewelry or even as a candy dish.

Sugar heart with royal border

Heart-shaped jewelry box

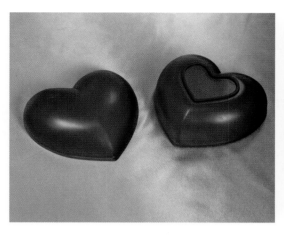

Mold the sugar heart in a heart candy mold or plastic dish.

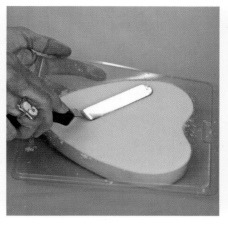

Pack the moist sugar firmly into each side of the mold. Level the sugar with an off set spatula.

For large molds place a cookie sheet on top of the molded sugar, hold it firmly with your hand and turn over.

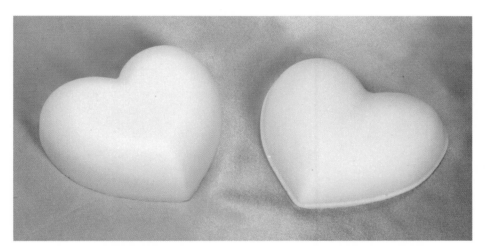

Remove the mold and leave the hearts on the tray to dry. Scrape the moist sugar from the inside of the heart leaving at least a 1/4 inch wall around the heart. Scrape the top portion thinner than the bottom half.

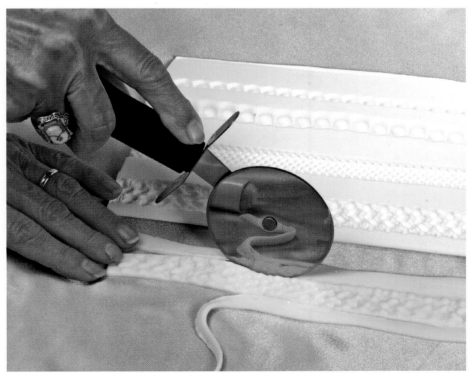

Roll a strip of fondant in a mold or free hand and trim with a pizza cutter if necessary. The piece should be about 3/4-inch wide.

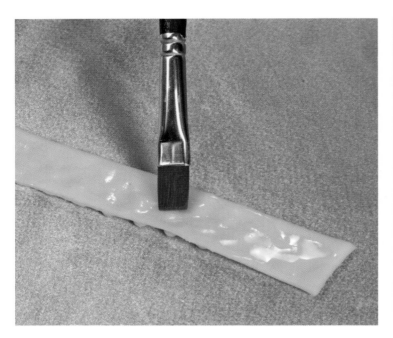

To attach the strip, moisten the back of it with a damp brush or add some royal frosting.

Place the strip inside of the bottom portion of the dish...

...allowing the piece to extend 1/4 inch above the molded heart.

If you are creating a box dish, gather a small piece of satin fabric with a needle and thread. Stuff it with a little fiberfill and attach to the bottom half of the heart box with a little royal icing after the heart is completely dry.

Place the top of the sugar box on a cookie sheet lined with waxed paper. Pipe a shell border around the edge of the heart with royal icing. Allow it to dry before removing the paper. Trim the top with small dots, a molded gum paste rose and leaves. Attach a small ribbon and bow.

To form a heart-shaped dish, mold a heart in a candy mold or in an individual cake pan. When removing the moist sugar leave a thicker area of sugar at the back of the dish to support the decorations. Finish the edge with royal icing reverse shells. Add satin ribbons and sugar flowers at the back. Individual sugar dishes can be used for sugar molded hearts for tea, coffee or Jordan almonds for a special party treat.

Two sizes of hearts with flowers

Heart-shaped candy dishes

### Heart Cake

Not only can the sugar hearts be used for boxes and candy dishes, the single heart, decorated like the lid of the candy box, can be used as the prominent decoration on a heart-shaped cake.

This would be perfect for Valentine Day, a bridal shower, Sweetheart's Day, or even a birthday.

Heart cake decorated with sugar heart. The cake was covered in soft pink fondant. Pearl luster was added to the lace top of the cake.

Close up of rose and border. The rose was molded of fondant in a silicone mold and the leaves cut with a plunger leaf cutter. There are small hearts around the bottom of the fondant covered board which were cut with a small heart cutter.

Place sugar heart onto lace overlay. The lace top is fondant molded in a lace mold designed by Carol Webb as is the fondant border. A cake pan was used to mark the heart shape. Decorative scissors were used to cut out the heart.

# Summer

In the heat of summer there are many occasions to celebrate that can be portrayed in molded sugar of one type or another, whether it be granulated, fondant, or gum paste. This summer we will celebrate Fathers Day, June brides, and a fun birthday cake for the Big Cheese.

### *Couch Potato*

This Fathers Day Couch Potato is perfect for the dad who likes to spend his free time laying on the couch, reading the paper, watching T.V., or sipping a cool drink. The couch can be made in advance, but the couch potato and throw must be added to the couch while they are still soft.

Couch Potato cake

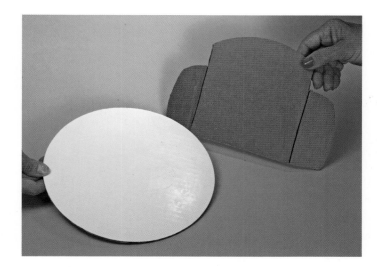

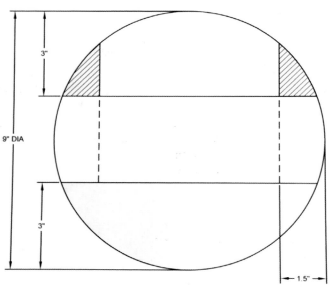

To form the couch in advance use a 9-inch cake circle. Place the circle with corrugated flutes running vertically and trace the design onto). Cut out and score on the lines indicated by the pattern. Score halfway through the cardboard and bend to form the sides of the couch.

Couch pattern

9" DIA
3"
3"
1.5"

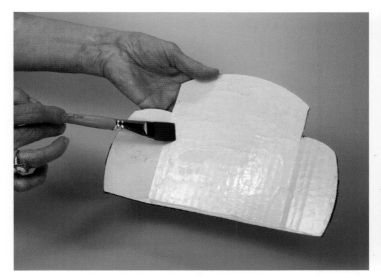

Moisten the cake circle with water.

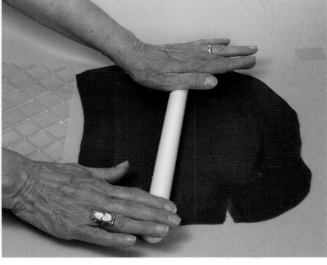

Use a rolling pin to roll out brown fondant and place it over the moist cardboard pattern. Roll it again to bring out the shape of the pattern.

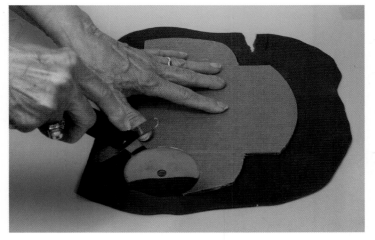

Turn the piece over and use a pizza cutter to trim off excess fondant.

Press the fondant so it sticks to the cardboard form.

Use a diamond impression mat to press a design into the fondant.

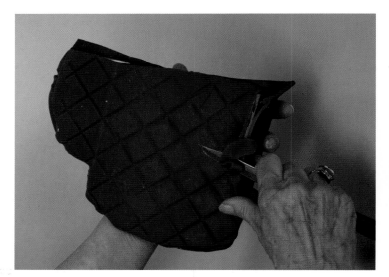

Cut another piece of the fondant to fit the back of the couch and add the diamond pattern to it. Dampen it and apply to the back of the couch. Trim around couch back

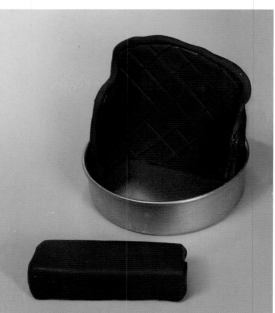

Fold in the sides of the couch and place it into a 7 inch cake pan. To prevent sticking, line the cake pan with waxed paper for easy removal. Moisten the edge of the couch.

Roll a long snake of chocolate fondant and apply it to the edge of the couch. Cut a piece of cake to fit the opening for the couch cushion. Cover the cushion in fondant the same color as the back of the couch.

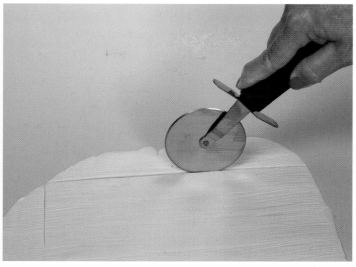

For the throw, roll out a thin layer of fondant that is approximately 6 inches x 8 inches. Use a textured rolling pin to impress a design into the throw.

Trim the throw with a pizza cutter.

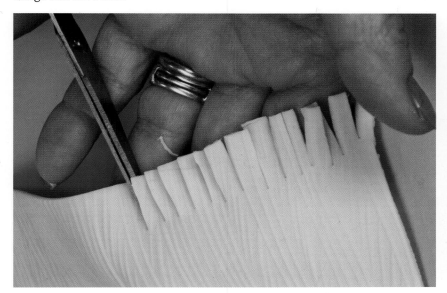

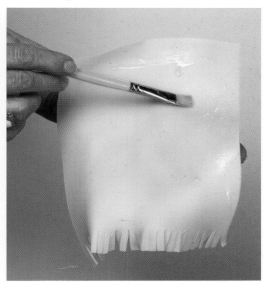

Clip the edge of the throw with scissors to form fringe.

Moisten the back of the throw with water.

Drape the throw over the end of the couch.

To form the couch potato, shape a ball of flesh colored fondant in the shape of an egg.

The arms are made by rolling long ovals of the yellow colored fondant and bent slightly. Rolled blue fondant is used for the legs.

Press an indentation in the lower half of each side of the potato for the legs. Press two more indentations higher on the body for placement of the arms.

To form the hands, shape two small teardrop shapes, flatten and cut a small "V" shape out for the thumb and press flat for the hands. Use a knife to make indentations for the fingers. Use the blunt end of a small object to make a slight indentation to place the hands at the end of the arms.

Roll a small oval for the nose. The eyes are tiny white ovals that are mashed flat. Cut the iris of the eyes from thin brown fondant using a #5 decorator tip. Add a black dot for the pupils with a black food safe pen or black pearls.

The shoes are small ovals of dark chocolate fondant. Use a ball tool to press indentations on the rear of the shoe so that it will fit onto the leg.

The beer can is a purchased cake decoration. To attach the parts, use water or gum glue. To form the couch potato mouth, press the wide end of a decorator tip into the couch potato head to form a partial circle for the mouth. Place small indentations in the head with a stylist for potato-like eyes.

Type your own personalized message and cut to fit the cake for the newspaper. Remove the paper before serving.

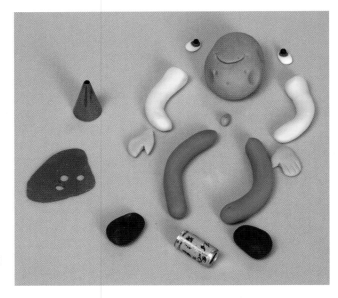

Couch potato and newspaper

Facial expressions

The cake and board are covered in fondant with a grosgrain ribbon border. The fondant covering on the board is textured.

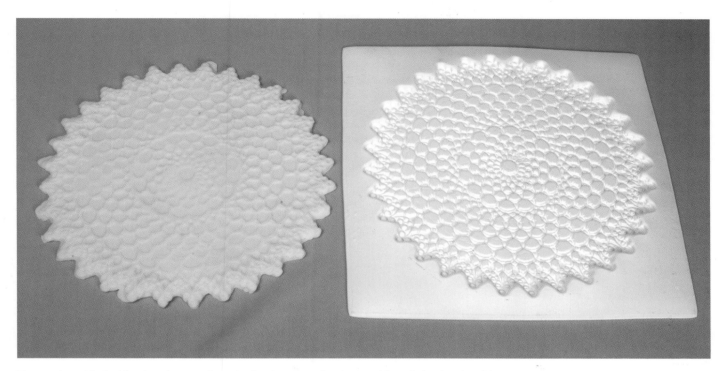

The rug is molded of fondant in a purchased cake decorator fondant mold made by Carol Webb.

If this doily mold is not available, you might be able to purchase plastic doilies at a dollar store, thrift store, or yard sale to use as an impression mat.

To color the rug, use powdered food colors and the dry brush technique. Always sample the color on a scrap piece of fondant. Dust the edge of the rug bringing color from the outside in. Make the center of the rug darker going in a circle with your color.

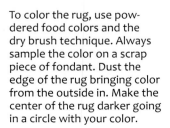

The sleepy dog is made by forming a tapered oval for the body. Form the body parts as described in the caption.

Hand molded dog

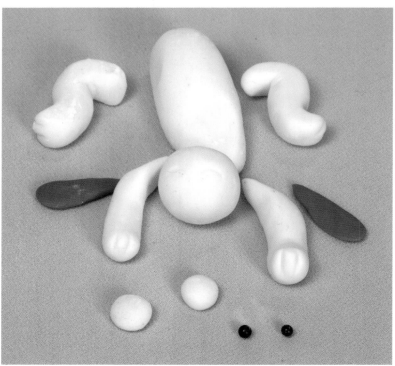

Make a tapered oval for the body.

Roll fondant logs for the legs. When you make legs and arms, roll a log and cut it in half to insure equal size of both limbs. Mark toe lines with the dull side of a knife. Attach the legs to the body with gum glue or water. Position the back legs so that they point backwards and the front legs are crossed.

Make a ball for the head and add it to the body. Roll two small balls and flatten them for the cheeks. Moisten the cheeks and apply to the head.

The nose is a black pearl. Sleepy eyes are formed with a #6, #7, or #8 decorator tip. The eyebrows and whisker marks are made with a food safe pen or a small paint brush and food color. The tongue is a tiny red fondant teardrop that has been flattened.

To form the tail, add a piece of chocolate fondant to a small snake of white fondant. Roll the two colors to combine and moisten with water or gum glue to attach to the dog body.

The ears are long teardrops that are flattened and added to the head with water or gum glue.

For the spots on the fur, roll chocolate fondant very thin and cut circles with the small end of a decorator tip. Moisten the spots and add to the body and legs of the dog. After adding the spots, use your fingertips to change the shapes so that they are random rather than perfectly round.

Dog bones are extremely easy to form and add so much interest to the cake.

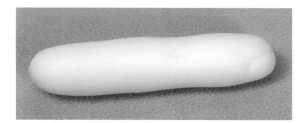

To form a bone, roll a fondant log that is approximately 3/4 inch in length.

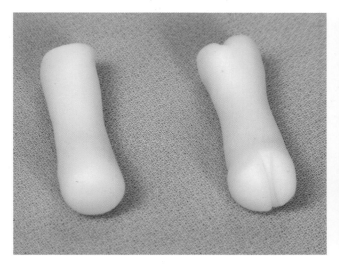

Roll it a little thinner in the center and make an indention in each end with the dull side of a knife to create the shape of a bone.

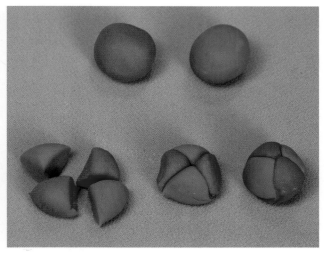

To form the two-colored ball make 2 equal size balls of fondant, one red and one blue. Cut each ball into quarters. Alternate the two colors for 4 sections of the ball. You will have two balls when you finish. Carefully roll into a ball without losing the shape or definition of colors.

To shape the pillow for your couch potato, roll out a thick piece of fondant that is about 1/3 inch thick.

Cover the fondant piece with clear plastic wrap and use a spatula to cut the pillow shape. The plastic wrap prevents sharp edges and rounds them over more like a pillow.

Arrange the couch potato and all of the pre-formed pieces onto the couch and place it on the braided rug in center of the cake. Arrange the newspaper, dog, bones and ball at appropriate positions. Fondant cut letters can be added to commemorate Fathers Day, a special birthday, or even retirement. Note: when heavy decorations are used, support should be added.

Use you fingers to soften the edge.

## *June Bride*

This huge sugar egg is proof that panorama eggs can be adapted for any season or occasion, and can be made in any size. This creation would certainly be recognized as a work of love for a wedding reception or bridal shower and it would surely be a conversation piece if the bride and groom were made to resemble the happy couple. This is a combination of molded granulated sugar, pastillage, fondant, and gum paste used to carry out our molded sugar theme.

A large 8 quart aluminum mixing bowl was selected to mold this large egg. It took 40 pounds of granulated sugar to mold the two halves (top and bottom) and the base, but much of this sugar was retrieved when the pieces were scraped out.

The two molded halves were turned out on plywood to provide stability and prevent cracking. A 9 inch oval cake pan was used to draw a pattern on paper for the opening in the egg. The paper was folded in half horizontally so half of the opening could be marked on each part of the egg. Damp paper towels were folded and cut to fit the pattern and laid on the opening area while the egg dried for several days. The towels were dampened every day.

Because both halves were molded in the same bowl, the top and bottom both had flat surface. The flat bottom worked well to set on the base. The flat top had to be built up with royal frosting to form a rounded base for the flowers. The base was formed in the bottom of the same bowl, but only molding the sugar about 3-4 inches deep. For support, a piece of cardboard was held against the sugar while it was being turned out.

The figures can be made well in advance or formed while you are waiting for the egg to completely dry. For the bride doll, tint a large ball of gum paste with flesh color for your ethnic preference. Work the paste until it is smooth and pliable. Smooth it into a narrow log and lay it into a gum paste doll mold. Press down and upward toward the top of the head, pressing the paste to pick up the facial features. Trim the paste until it is flush with the top surface of the mold. Repeat this process for the back half of the mold. Remove the back half from the mold and lay it on a bed of cotton. Brush it with gum glue and place a short skewer vertically in the bodice. Gently remove the front mold being careful not to distort the neck and face. Place the front body onto the back half over the skewer. Smooth the seams and position the head. Leave it to dry. When the piece is thoroughly dry, tint some flesh color royal icing and fill in any cracks in the seams. Smooth with your fingertip.

These are plaster molds that have very good detailed facial features, but they also scratch very easily. There are many plastic molds on the market.

The lower body is formed from pastillage. It dries fast, it is stronger than gum paste and is less expensive. Work the pastillage until it is very smooth. Form it into a narrow log. Thin the waist area to match the base of the doll mold. Insert a skewer into the soft paste and remove in order to leave a hole to later attach the torso.

Gum paste bride

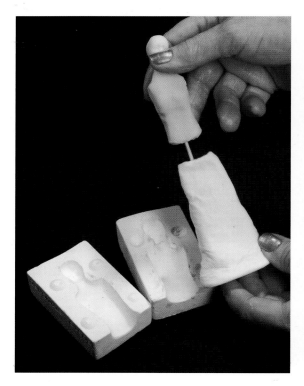

When the two pieces are dry, insert the skewer into the pastillage base and connect the two pieces, securing with royal icing.

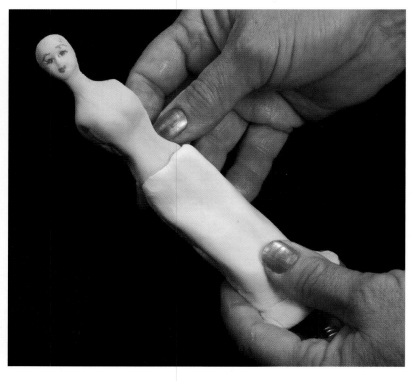

Connect to base and add makeup

Cut a fondant bodice for the doll, dampen around the seams and attach to the doll. It is difficult to give a precise pattern for the dress bodice because of the various sizes of molds and designs of dress, but if you have ever used a pattern to sew a dress or played with paper dolls, this task will be easier.

Some commercial molds have sections for the arms, but this one does not and the hand-molded arms are very delicate and realistic. The arms should be formed from the same flesh colored paste used for the face. Start with a small ball and roll it into a log that is approximately the right size. The length of the arm is twice the length from the shoulder to the waist. The hand is the length from the chin to the middle of the forehead. Mark and score the little log in half for the elbow and mark the lower area in half again to mark the wrist. Flatten the end of the log for a hand. Shape the arm, using your own as a guide. Roll the arm between your fingers to narrow and shape the wrist and elbow.

Shaping the hand is the most difficult part of the figure but patience will pay off. Small manicure scissors are excellent to cut fingers apart. Cut a "V" shaped section to separate the thumb from the fingers. Score the finger area in half and mark each half again to ensure that you have four equal size fingers. Roll the tiny fingers between yours to give them a natural look. Avoid having the hands in a straight, stiff position. Separate the fingers and shape them into a more natural position. Use your own hand as a guide.

When the hand is complete and dry, paint each nail with a tiny brush and red or pink food color for nail polish. If the arm has become too long during the procedure, cut off the excess at an angle to fit the shoulder. You must decide what position your finished arms will be in. Hold an arm against your gum paste body to get an idea how it will lie. Place the arms in the correct position on a bed of cotton to dry.

When the figure is completely dry, apply the facial features in much the same manner as you would makeup. If you want to highlight the cheekbones, use a "Q" tip to apply a little blush. With a white pencil or a little white food color, fill in the eye area. Use a colored pencil to form the iris of the eye. Hold the pencil where you wish the iris to be and go around in a tiny circle to obtain sufficient color, blue, brown or green. Use a #3 or #4 hard lead pencil to make a small black dot for the pupil in the center of the iris. Use the same pencil to outline the top half of the eye, around and under the iris. The line should not extend to the corners of the eye. Apply eyelashes to the outer corners of the eye and only to the upper eyelid using the same pencil. Add the eyebrows by using a soft brown pencil. With a pink or red pencil or tiny amount of food color, color the lips. Make a tiny dot inside each nostril with a pink pencil.

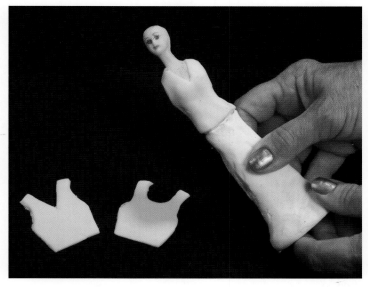

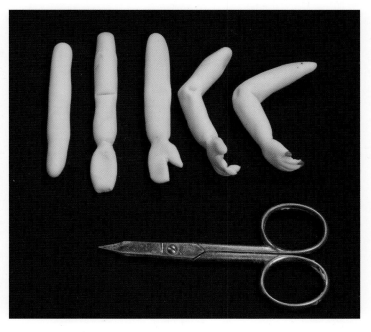

Steps for arms

Frequently, the hair is added with tinted royal icing, but, in this instance, we have used brown fondant. Lay a gum ball-size piece of brown fondant in the palm of your hand and push a small gum ball, that is approximately the size of the doll head, into the fondant to form a cup shape.

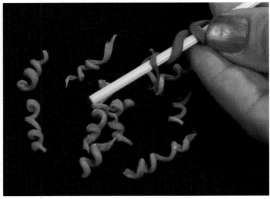

Remove the gum ball and place the cup over the head of the bride doll. Slightly dampen the skull cap to adhere to the doll head. Form hair lines with a modeling tool or the dull side of a table knife. Press the tool into the soft paste and pull down to blend the hair onto the neck and face.

The curls are formed by rolling tiny pieces of brown fondant around a toothpick or small skewer. Remove the curls from the toothpick before they are completely dry. Slightly dampen the top of the curl and press it into the soft skull cap. Start at the lower part of the back of the head and work upward in rows of curls. Arrange to form the hair style that you are attempting to achieve.

There are limitless designs for dress and skirts. For this pleated design, roll a large piece of fondant very thin then roll again with a fabric textured impression roller. Measure the length from the waist to the feet and cut the skirt that length with a pizza cutter. To form a pleated skirt, alternate layers of skewers that is one skewer under the fondant, the next skewer on top of the fondant, and the next under the fondant until you complete the piece in this manner. (The same pleating technique is used for the ruffle on the bridal egg. You will find it illustrated on page 79.) Gently remove the skewers and pinch the pleats together at the top edge. Use a small roller to flatten out the top edge and secure the pleats.

Pleated skirt with sequins & pearls

Pattern for the bridal gown

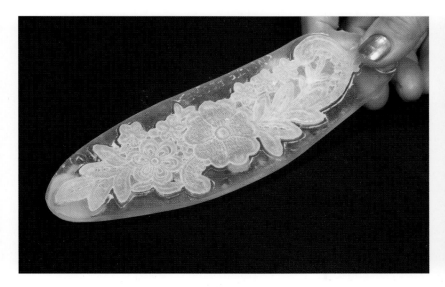

Mold fondant lace pieces in a silicone mold. Dampen the back side slightly and apply around the bottom edge of the skirt. Dampen the waist of the doll and attach the skirt.

To form tiny sugar pearls, roll out a thin piece of white fondant. Cut individual pearls with the small end of a #2 decorator tip. Roll each pearl in your hand to form a smooth ball and drop into a bottle with a small amount of pearl luster. Shake the jar frequently to coat the pearls and to prevent them from sticking. Brush a small amount of piping gel where you want the pearls and put them in place with a pair of tweezers.

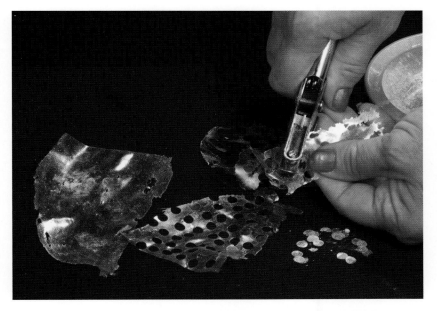

The sequins are very appropriate for wedding dresses, as many are adorned by sequins. Mix 1 tablespoon of powdered unflavored gelatin with 3 tablespoons water. Let the mixture "bloom," then heat it in the microwave a few seconds until dissolved and clear. Brush the mixture on a cookie sheet in a thin layer. Let the gelatin dry thoroughly and it will easily peel off. Brush the sheet with a light dusting of dry pearl luster. Use a paper punch to cut numerous sequins from the gelatin sheet. Add to the dress with piping gel. The luster gives them an iridescent sheen.

Add the fondant curls to the head and style as you desire. Tightly gather a piece of fabric tulle with a needle and thread. Place the gathered part on top of the bride's head and secure with a little royal icing.

Place a fondant, pearl covered tiara on top of the head over the area when the veil is secured.

Attach the gathered sleeves around the armholes of the dress and trim the edges with pearls.

To form the flower in the brides hand, place a tiny piece of yellow fondant on the end of a 2 inch fine wire. Roll the yellow around the wire to form the center of the flower. Wrap a tiny, teardrop shape of white fondant around the point of a skewer to form the calla lily blossom. When this dries, slip the wire through the base of the lily and wrap floral tape around the stem. The yellow tip of the wire will be inside of the calla lily.

The bow at the waist on the back of the dress is formed from white fondant. Roll a thin strip and texture before cutting the strip 1 inch wide. Fold each end to the center to form loops. Prop them open slightly with tissue until they dry. Add to the back of the dress with a little royal icing.

Brush the entire dress with pearl luster.

Every bride needs a groom and this is no exception. This groom is molded free hand with the exception of a face mold. Roll a medium size ball of flesh color gum paste and rub it into a smooth ball. Brush the facial area with a touch of cornstarch and press it into the face mold. Use your thumb to apply pressure at the base of the skull. Press it into the mold and up to assure detailed facial features. With your fingertip, smooth the thumb print and mold the back of the head into a rounded shape. If this area is rough, do not worry about it because it will later be covered with hair. Insert a toothpick and gently remove the head from the mold and prop to dry.

The male body is easily formed from pastillage. Roll a log the approximate size that you want the finished body. The body is normally seven times the length of the head. Flatten a log of pastillage slightly. Trim the top edges for the shoulder area. Roll the log between your fingers to form the waist. Cut the bottom of the log into half to form the legs. Starting at the bottom of the foot, insert a skewer up through each leg into the upper torso to support the standing figure. Form each leg into a rounded shape. If the legs seem too long, simply cut them off. Form a foot at the base of each leg, making sure that the sole of the foot is smooth and flat. Prop the figure in a standing posi-

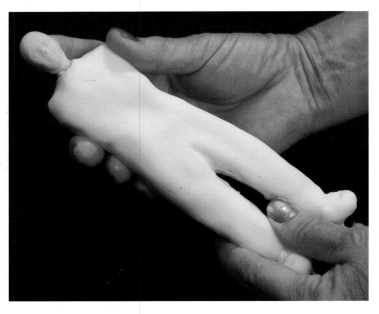

Mold groom figure

tion to assure that he will stand straight. Insert the toothpick of the head into the soft pastillage body. When the head is dry, apply facial features. Remember, that the male hands are larger with stubbier fingers than the lady's.

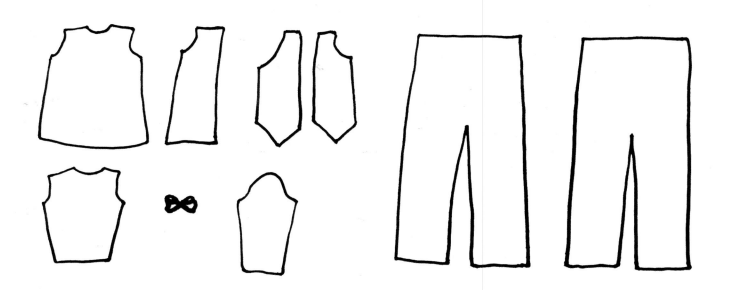

Patterns for the groom's clothing

Clothing for the groom can be made from gum paste or fondant. Only the front area of the shirt will show so it is not necessary to make the complete piece. Cut a piece of white and add it to the chest of the groom with a touch of water or gum glue. Add a narrow strip for the collar. Two "V"-shaped coral color strips are added over the shirt for the vest.

For the shoes use black paste to cover the top of the shoe. Apply a narrow strip of black around the sides of the foot. The pants are long enough to fit from the waist to the ankle and wide enough to wrap around your figure. Cut out the approximate size to fit the back. Brush gum glue at the waist, side seams and inseams. Trim the piece to fit and repeat for the front of the pants.

The coat is cut from the same black paste. Attach the back at the shoulder and side seams. The front of the jacket is applied in two pieces over the shirt and vest. Lay the top front edges back to form the lapel. Trim any excess and smooth the side and shoulder seams. Make sure to clip and leave the armholes free. Glue a tiny black strip around the neck for the jacket collar. Form a tiny black tie and attach.

Cut the sleeve. Wrap it around the arm securing the seam on the underside with gum glue. It may be necessary to clip a small "V" shape from the elbow area so the sleeve will lie smoothly on the arm. Secure the arms as described for the bride. Add hair and a tiny calla lily boutonniere.

The groom can be attached directly on the cake with royal frosting or he can be attached to a small, dried, round of pastillage for easy removal.

Dressed groom

Glue the base and the lower half of the egg together with royal and let dry completely.

Most of the scene inside the egg can be created before assembly. Brush any excess sugar from the inside before adding royal icing greenery. (Remember that the eggs can be lined with fondant to make them extra easy to paint or decorate.)

Add royal icing grass to the lower half of the egg. Paint the upper half or sky of the egg with light blue royal. Brown royal tree trunks and foliage are added.

Inside the panorama egg

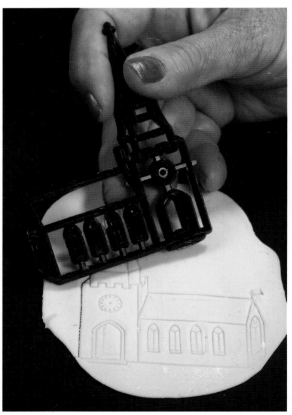

The focal point inside the egg is the church in the distance. It is made from a patchwork cutter. Roll the fondant thinly and impress the church design. Trim the excess.

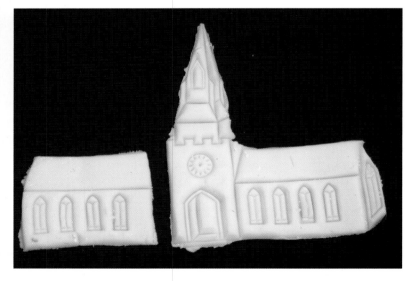

An extra end was cut to make this church longer. After the church is dried, paint with food color and secure inside the egg up on the hill. Miniature marshmallows can be fastened to the back of the church to hold it away from the wall of the egg and give it more of a three-dimensional appearance.

For the path, mix brown, black and white fondant to get a marbleized pattern. Roll the fondant out and press firmly into a cobblestone impression mat. Trim the edges. The path will be wider at the opening of the egg and wind and narrow in the distance. Place in the bottom of the egg leading up to the church.

Arrange the couple in the base of the egg. Pipe white royal icing around the edge of the lower egg and place the top egg into the fresh royal.

To conceal the connection seams cover them with fondant ruffles.

Roll out a strip of coral fondant and roll with a fabric design impression roller. Cut 2 inch wide ribbon strips.

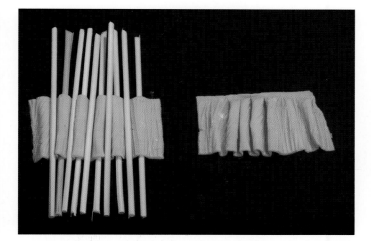

To form the ruffle use skewers. This is the same method that was used to pleat the bridal skirt. Place one skewer on top of the ruffle, the second skewer under the fondant, the third on top, and the fourth under and continue this pattern for the length of the ruffle. Remove the skewers and press one edge together and roll with a small roller or a skewer. Ruffle enough fondant to encircle the egg.

Fasten the flattened edge at the seam with the ruffle edge down and fasten with royal. Repeat this process and fasten with the ruffle edge up around the seam.

Mold coral pearls in a bead maker and secure them in the center of the seam where the two ruffles meet. Brush with pearl luster. Form more ruffles for the base of the egg as pictured. Pipe a royal icing shell border around the opening of the egg.

Form the flowers in advance so they have time to dry. The stephanotis is a tiny flower that is very dainty and lovely; they are frequently used in bridal bouquets.

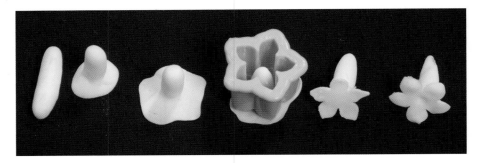

Roll a small cone of white paste. Flatten one end with your thumb and forefinger like a little pancake. Roll this flat piece out on the table so the little log is still attached and up in the air. Place a cutter over the log and cut the blossom from the rolled out paste. Lay the blossom on a cel pad and use a small ball tool to cup the back of each petal. Hollow the center with a skewer or handle of a small paint brush.

To form the calla lilies roll the paste thinly and cut the flowers with a calla lily cutter or template. Lay the piece on a cel pad and soften the upper half of the flower with a ball tool. Roll one side of the base over to the other side and attach with a dot of gum glue. Small, pointed paper drinking cups are perfect to use as drying supports if available. Turn the cup upside down and insert the pointed tip into the lily throat. Roll the side edges with a cocktail stick or your fingers for more shape. For the centers, roll a small log of yellow paste. Brush it with gum glue and roll in finely ground corn meal. Insert the stamen into the throat of the dried lily and secure with a small amount of royal.

Cut the petals of the coral roses, soften the edges, dry and assemble as described for the roses on the Royal Egg. Brush with a mixture of coral dusting powder and pearl luster.

Arrange three large roses on top of the
egg and let the floral arrangement cas-
cade around both sides of the panorama opening. The design can be made
in any color to complement the bridal
theme and the couple can be dressed
to match the bride and groom.

Couple inside egg

## The Big Cheese

This is a very simple cake but the hand molded mice make it extremely popular as the centerpiece for numerous occasions. It is particularly cute to inscribe a message "The Big Cheese Continues to Age."

Frost a two-layer cake and cover with yellow fondant. Use a round measuring spoon to press indentations in the fondant to create the appearance of cheese. If you are using butter cream icing, let it crust and dip a measuring spoon in hot water then press into the icing to form holes. Do not press too hard, but only enough to form deep indentions.

Forming holes in cheese

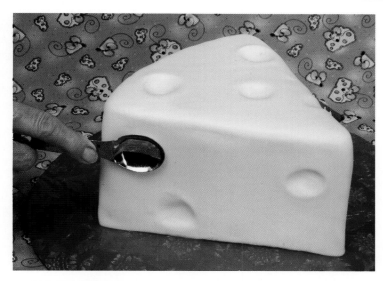

To form the body of the mouse, dust an egg pan or an egg-shaped candy mold with corn starch so that the fondant will not stick.

Press gray fondant into the mold to form the body of the mouse.

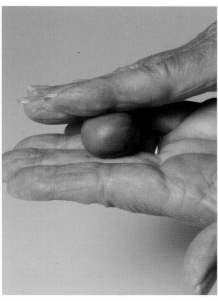
Roll an egg shape for the head of the mouse.

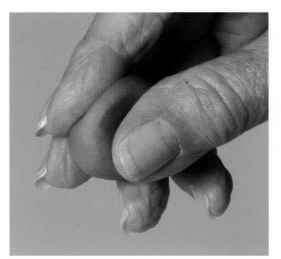
Pinch the egg shape to make a more realistic shape for the mouse head. Add a piece of spaghetti to the head for support.

Form the ears. If you make the ears in advance and let them dry, they will be easier to add to the head.

The basic forms for a standing mouse and a walking mouse.

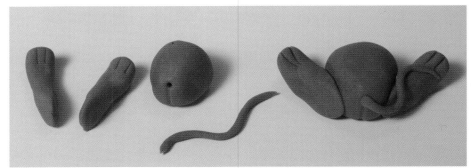

The parts and assembly of the back half of a mouse

The parts for the sitting mouse, including arms, legs and other body parts. Roll white fondant out thin and cut a small oval with a cutter for the belly of the mouse.

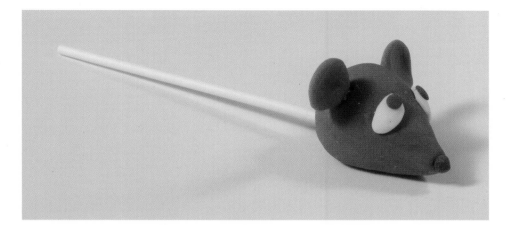

To display a head poking from a hole in the cake, complete the head as previously described then add a sucker stick into the head...

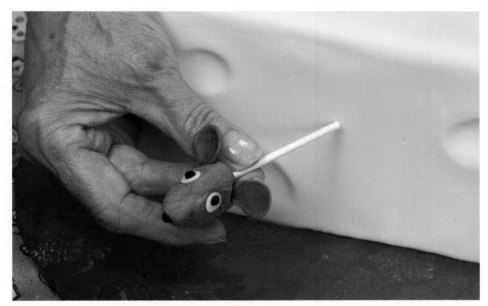

... and insert it into the cake.

If you prefer not to hand mold your mice, you can mold one in a candy mold and brush with powdered color.

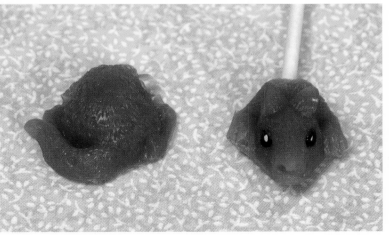

A second option would be to purchase gummy mice from a discount store. You can cut a slit in the head of the gummy mouse and insert a small sucker stick to help it stay in place.

Arrange the mice in various position such as one sitting up mouse and the back half or the head going in or out of the cake. The large mouse head was made on a sucker.

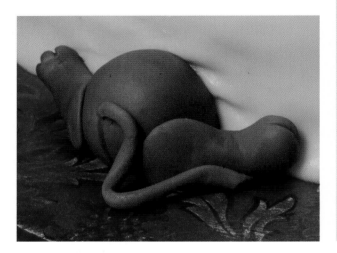

Mouse going into cheese

Gummy mouse in cake

Mouse sitting against the cake

# Fall

In our area of the country, fall is one of the most beautiful times of the year — the leaves turn hues of gold, orange, and yellow and brush the rolling hills like an artist's canvas. Fall is a fun time for the children with the festivities of Halloween and a time for thanks and families gathering for Thanksgiving, so we are concentrating on these two occasions.

# *Halloween*

Halloween characters

To form the rustic fence, roll out brown fondant or gum paste to a medium thickness. Roll a textured rolling pin over the fondant to add texture. If you do not have this type of rolling pin you could use a tooth pick to scratch the surface. Cut strips and use water to attach the pieces. Do not make the fence straight. Make it a little curved and let it dry. Paint the fence with food color then wipe off the excess with a tissue to give a weathered look.

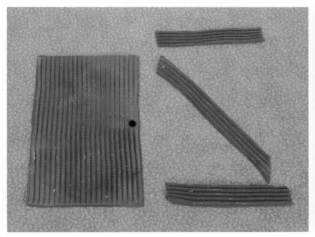

The door is made by lightly mixing tan and a small amount of brown together. Do not mix the colors well, but leave them marbled. Roll out the fondant and cut a door 3-1/4 inches by 4-3/4 inches. Cut strips for accent pieces and use a black fondant pearl for the door knob.

Mix some black and white fondant together to make a marble effect for the side walk. Press the fondant into a cobblestone mold to get the textured walk. Cut the walk to shape with a pizza cutter.

The tree stump is four 6 inch cake layers.

Stack two layers together and add straws for support.

Place the next two layers on a cake board and add to the first two. Drive a skewer down through all four layers to add support.

Frost the cake with brown butter cream and take a decorator's comb to give the impression of bark on the tree.

With a #16 decorator tip and brown icing, add roots and a knot hole.

The adorable little bear is dressed for the occasion in her little black witch's costume.

Make a center cone about 1-1/2 inch by 3-1/2 inch from scrap fondant. Make a hole with a straw so that you can attach the head. Let the piece dry. Cut a circle from black fondant large enough to cover the base. Trim the edge with decorative scissors. Cut, remove, and discard 1/4 of the circle. Moisten it with water and wrap around the base allowing the dress to stand away from the base. Cut a circle of purple fondant with a decorative cutter for the collar. Make the head by rolling brown fondant over a gum ball leaving room to place a sucker stick in the head to attach to the body. Form a small hole in the gum ball and insert the sucker stick for added support. Make the muzzle from light brown or cream colored fondant. The eyes are black fondant pearls. For the hat roll a long tear drop into a Mexican hat shape. Thin the edges for a slight ruffle effect. The arms are made my rolling smaller tear drop shapes and using a ball tool to open them slightly. Roll two small balls into a short tear drop shape to form the paws. Use the back side of a knife to make the paw marks. Insert into the arm. Add a piece of spaghetti for support and attach with a little water or royal icing.

To form the flames, twist orange, yellow, and red fondant together. Roll it out and cut flames with a heart cutter. Cut each in half and pull slightly with a little twist for the flickering flames.

For the caldron roll black fondant around a large gum ball. Flatten the bottom so it will sit flat. Roll a long rope for the top lip on the caldron. The logs are large pretzels, though Tootsie Roll candies could be used.

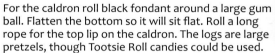

Flames on the caldron.

To form a Jack-O-Lantern add orange fondant to a gum ball.

Use the blunt side of a knife to add the lines to the pumpkin. Use a calyx cutter to cut out green fondant for the top of the pumpkin. Add a brown fondant stem.

To make the bear wearing the pumpkin costume, make the pumpkin as described above and add the legs, arms, and head to the pumpkin. The calyx sits on top of the bear head.

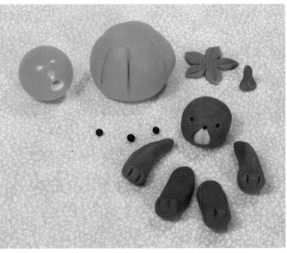

Pieces for a pumpkin bear

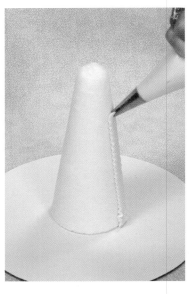

The corn shock is piped over a sugar mold that was molded in a plastic champagne flute. Glass containers do not work well for molds, as the sugar will frequently stick.

Cream colored royal icing is piped using a leaf tip to form the corn stalks.

Allow the shock to dry before adding to the scene.

Press a ball of fondant into a plastic bell mold and use the shape of the bell to form the main costume of the ghost. Flair and thin the edge of the ghost sheet.

Form the head of the ghost over a small sucker with part of the stick cut off. Shape the fondant in a tapered oval for the body. Press the cut off stick with the head into the body. Shape two smaller pointed ovals for the arms. Open them up with a gum paste tool or a paint brush handle. The small tapered balls are used for hands. Spaghetti was added to help them stay in place. Roll out black fondant and cut small circles with a #7 or #8 decorator tip for the eyes. Cut one more and roll it out to form the mouth.

Press the dried body of the ghost into the costume and shape the fondant around the dried form. Add the arms, hands and face features by applying a small amount of water.

## *Fruitful Harvest*
### Leigh Sipe, Guest Artist

The Fruitful Harvest cake was designed and cre-ated by guest decorator Leigh Sipe of Harrodsburg, Kentucky. Leigh was gracious and generous enough to attend our photo shoots and pitch in wherever she needed to be of assistance, and usually we needed a lot of assistance in the midst of our turmoil. She is a talented deco-rator who owns her own custom design business known as *Cakes by Leigh*. She is very active in I.C.E.S. and has served two terms as the Kentucky State Representative. Leigh has been a close friend to both of us for many years and we wanted to devote this section especially to her. Thanks Leigh!

Fruitful Harvest

The basket weave roller was not designed to be disassembled, but the old saying is that necessity is the mother of invention. So, when Leigh needed a short roller, she set about finding a way to break the large roller into smaller sections.

At the hardware store purchase various lengths of all thread bolts that will fit in the same hole where you removed the original one. You will also need washers and wing nuts for each size. If you have a variety of bolts you can assemble the roller into the appropriate size for your cake whether it is 2 inch tall, 4 inch or any size. Leigh loves this roller so much that she keeps one for chocolate frosting and one for white.

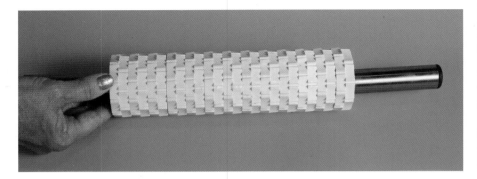

The "Deep Basket Weave Roller" is a PME product available from Beryl's as well as CK. There are numerous lengths and diameters of these basket weave rollers. This one is about 2-1/2 inches in diameter and is made up of several segments.

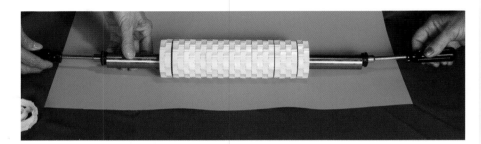

This roller has a hex-head bolt on each end of the roller to secure the segments together. You need two of the same size hex-head screw drivers, one for each end. This is a much easier process if two people work together. (If you are not sure about the size screw driver that should be used to take the piece apart, go to your local hardware store and let the clerk help you match up the size.) Be sure to save the original bolts and all the pieces so that you can reassemble. You need the larger roller in tact for big pieces of fondant.

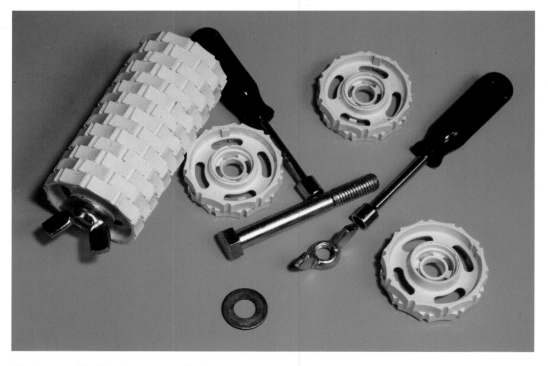

The disassembled basket weave roller. Rejoin segments to make it the right size for the sides of the cake, and replace the handles with a bolt and a wing nut at one end to hold the roller together.

Frost the entire cake with butter cream frosting. Allow the frosting to dry, then smooth it with a paper towel.

When the frosting has crusted, hold the short roller against the side of the cake, press firmly and move the roller around the circumference of the cake.

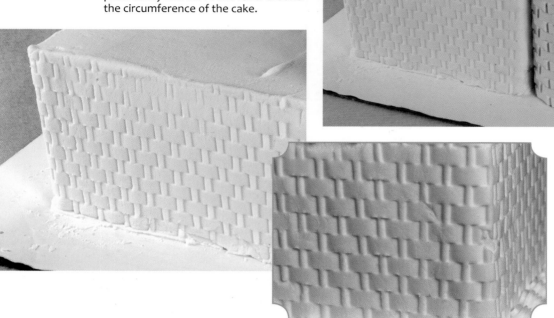

The roller creates a beautiful basket weave design on the cake without all the work of piping.

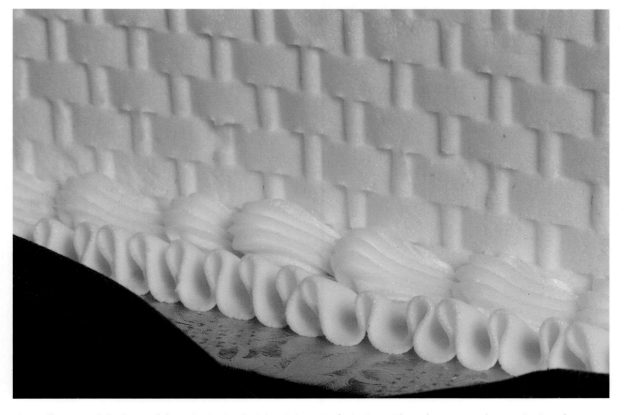

The ruffle around the base of the cake is piped with a Bakery Craft tip #070. They also carry a shorter tip #050 but Leigh prefers the longer one for borders. Above the ruffle pipe a star tip #18 -21 in a shell design.

The focal point of this cake is the chocolate molded cornucopia and the colorful fruit. These are all molded with colored chocolate in various fruit shaped two-piece candy molds. The grapes were purchased in white from Cal-Java and brushed with the appropriate shade of dusting powder. You can form these from tiny balls of fondant if you prefer to mold your own. Berries can also be molded but these are Jelly Belly Raspberry and Blackberries purchased from Cracker Barrel.

The chocolate cornucopia and fruit.

Fondant leaves are nestled amid the fruit for a colorful fall effect.

Pipe a dot of frosting on the back of each leaf and arrange it on the cake. Arrange the fruit and leaves on top of the completed cake to appear as though they are flowing from the cornucopia.

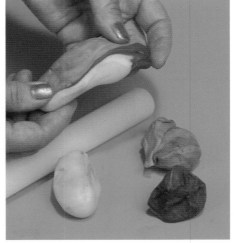

Color several balls of fondant in fall colors — red, orange, yellow, rust, and green. Pinch a marble-sized ball from two or three of the colors. Roll these balls to blend the colors and roll out the blended ball.

Vein & cutter tools

Cut out a leaf with a gum paste leaf cutter. Cookie cutters make excellent leaf cutters and are easy to find in maple or oak leaves. Look at the back side of the leaf, as frequently the back has a prettier blend than the front. Imprint veins with the dull side of a table knife or a purchased leaf veiner.

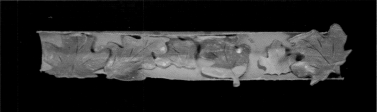

Place the leaf in a flower former to dry in a curved position. Allow the leaves to dry overnight.

When they retain their shape brush the leaves with a rust or copper dusting powder or luster dust.

# Winter

Winter completes the cycle of decorating with molded designs. It is a fun season as our puppies frolic on the ice. Even the penguins join in as they have a winter wonderland wedding.

# *Ice Skating Puppies*

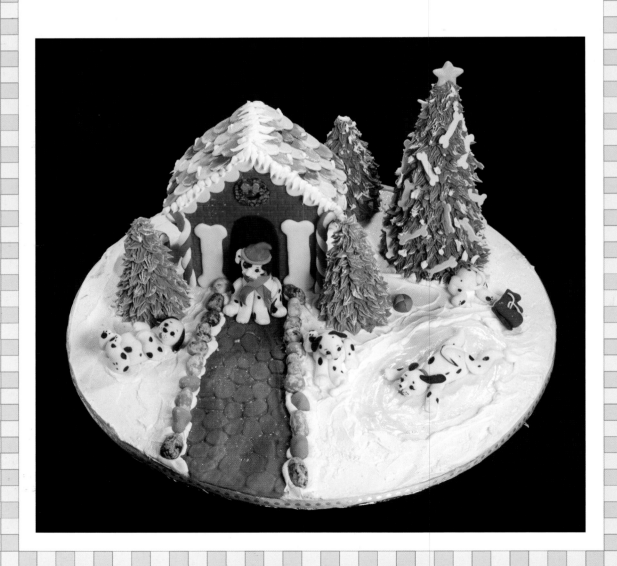

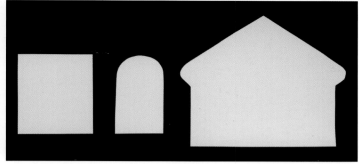

...and cut them out.

Trace around the dog house cake pan
to make patterns on parchment paper ...

Frost the cake with red icing and place it on a large
cake drum which is 16 to 18 inches.

Drive a dowel through the cake and
into the cake board to assure that the
house will stand in an upright position.

Two types of brick impression molds
for fondant.

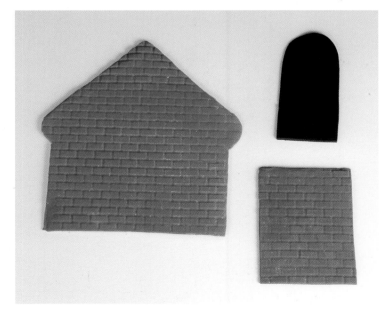

Cut pieces of red fondant using the patterns and press the brick pattern into the
fondant. Moisten the back and add the
pieces to the iced cake. Use red and white
twisted fondant to each corner of the dog
house to cover the area where the pieces
of fondant join.

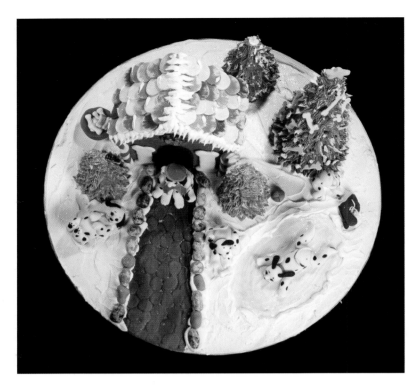

Add a thin layer of icing on the roof. Add colored fondant circles which have been cut with the large end of a 2D decorator tip. Use white food coloring to resemble snow on the tiles and trees, using a dry brush technique.

Tiny fondant dog bones are a delightful touch to the scene.

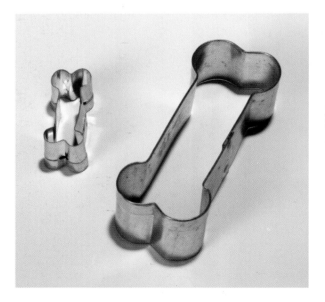

They can be molded free hand or cut with a gum paste or cookie cutter such as the small one pictured and shaped by hand. The smaller bones on this cake are made of gum paste and the larger ones from fondant. The larger cutter was used to form the large bone shapes on either side of the dog house door.

To form the bowl, roll a ball of red fondant smoothly in your hand.

Use a medium size gum ball to press an indention in the red ball of fondant to form the dish. Remove the gum ball and fill the cavity with little dog bones.

The parts for the little puppy on his back. Spaghetti is used to aid in holding the legs in place. Black fondant pearls are used for the eyes. Mix a small amount of black fondant with some white and roll a snake shape for the tail. Two small balls are flattened for the snout. The nose is a white tear drop shape with a black tip.

A food pen is used to color dots on the puppies.

A red fondant tear drop is used for the tongue.

The same basic pieces can be used to make a variety of puppies that can be arranged in any position. The various shapes add personality to the cake.

The little puppy falling on the ice has his front feet stretched out in front of him and the back legs stretched backward as though he has lost complete control of his footing. The frozen pond is a little pale blue royal icing added to the board. Piping gel is added to the dried royal to represent the ice.

The puppy that is sitting down scratching his ear with his little paw has a look of amazement on his face as if he is wondering why he can't stand up on the ice.

The puppy going under the tree is only the rear half of the dog with extra greenery added over the connection to conceal the fact that the head really isn't hidden under the tree.

The body of the larger dog in front of the house is shaped with a small gum ball inside. The front legs are long and straight except for the feet. Mark the toes with the back side of a knife. One ear is black. The other ear is white and curled slightly to give it more shape. Two round balls flattened slightly form the face. The red and green rope scarf was twisted and rolled out then cut with a pizza cutter. Scissors were used to cut the fringe. The hat is shaped like a Hershey Kiss pulled to a point. Place the red cone on a circle of green and shape to the head of the dog. The wreath over the dog house door is formed in a candy mold painted then some of the color is wiped off with a tissue.

Numerous trees can be scattered around your dog house to give it an outdoor appearance. Position the trees around the dog house and secure in white royal icing snow. Some of the trees have been decorated with tiny red fondant balls and miniature dog bones to add a festive touch of the holidays.

The largest tree was shaped in a large Mylar cone mold, while others were made using an ice cream cone base.

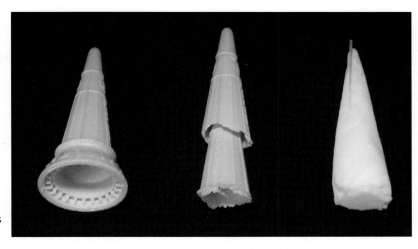

The trees can be frosted over pointed ice cream cones or sugar molded trees. For a taller tree you can stack two pointed cones together.

Green royal icing is piped to cover the trees. It can be piped with a leaf tip or a small star tip. Start at the base of the cone and work in a circular pattern until you reach the top. When the frosting dries, brush some of the areas lightly with royal icing...

...and sprinkle generously with edible glitter.

Every little puppy loves to chew on an old shoe, so we have provided one for our group of puppies. Roll out brown fondant and shape it to form a "L" shape for the shoe. Use a brush handle to open up the top part of the shoe. Roll a small piece of darker brown for the sole. Do not glue the sole all the way on so it will look like the sole is coming off.

The walk way is made with black and white marbleized fondant that is placed in a mold to form cobblestones. Candy rocks are added to the sides of the sidewalk. Add extra white royal snow where needed and sprinkle the damp snow generously with edible glitter.

## Snow Balls

*Opposite, top:*
Snow ball with Ginger Bread man scene. The holly is cut with a gum paste plunger cutter. The rose is molded in a silicone mold. Trees are molded in a candy mold and the ginger bread man is made of fondant.

Another snow ball with a snow man scene.

*Opposite, bottom:*
Small, medium, and large snow balls.

A gelatin mold is used to form the sugar base for the snow balls. If the base mold does not have an indention in the center, scoop out some of the sugar as soon as you turn out the mold. This gives a place for the egg to set. Do not scrape out the inside of the base as you need the weight for stability.

There are many things that can serve as ball molds, including Christmas decorations.

Plastic candy molds can also be used to mold the ball. Use the mold to make a sugar ball as was done with the egg mold earlier. Let the sugar mold dry thoroughly.

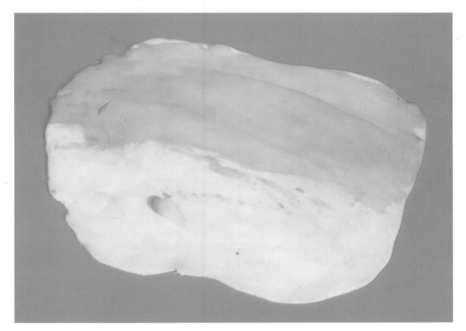

The inside of the snow ball is lined with fondant. Roll out fondant until it is very thin and dust the top with dry blue food powder.

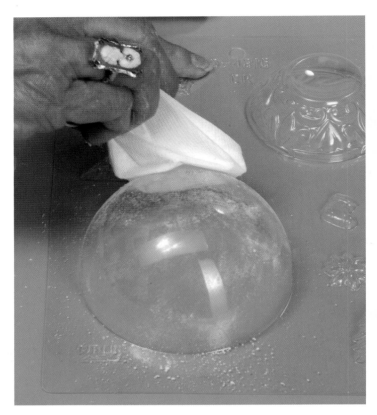

Dust the back side of the ball mold with corn starch. Doing this makes it easier to shape the fondant to the inside of the sugar ball.

Place the colored side of the fondant down over the mold and smooth over the ball.

Trim around the edge with a pizza cutter and carefully remove the fondant from the back of the mold

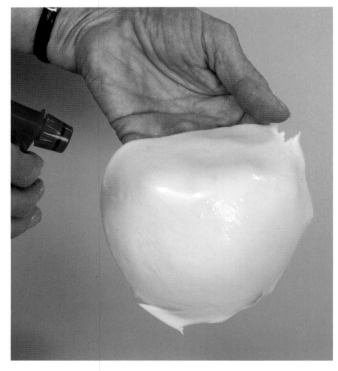

Spray the fondant with a little water to dampen it.

Place the fondant inside the dried sugar ball, smooth and trim the edges.

Trim the excess fondant from the edge of the ball

Paint the fence and tree directly into the fondant lined ball with Vodka and food colors. The alcohol dries quickly and leaves the color without the moisture.

The result

Candy molds can be used for the standing figures in the snow ball. This mold has both trees and a snow man.

Dust the inside of a candy mold with cornstarch.

Mold the snowman and tree using fondant. When you are molding fondant in candy molds, the mold must be dusted with corn starch.

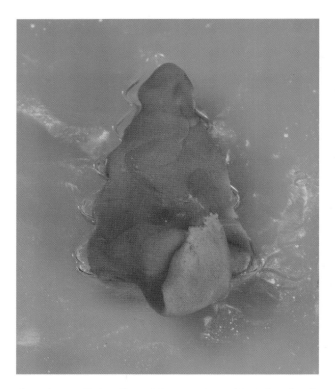

If you leave a little tail to stick up on the molded piece it will help you to remove it from the mold.

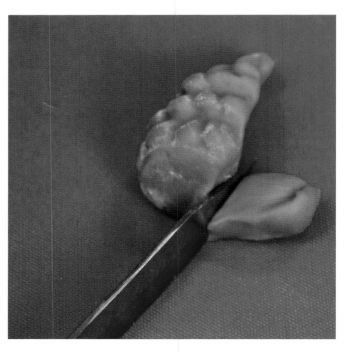

You can always cut off any excess.

Paint the figure and tree.

Give the tree an antiquing effect by wiping off the excess paint with a tissue. Darker paint stays in the cracks and crevices of the tree.

Add touches of white frosting with a brush to resemble snow.

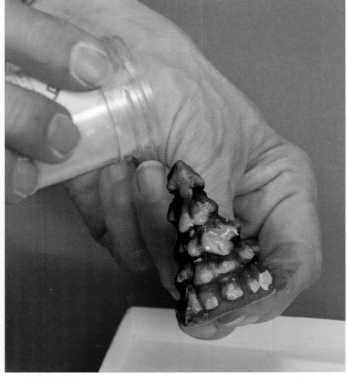

Add edible glitter to the snow while the royal icing is still damp.

To shape the gingerbread man, hand mold a long tear drop shape and cut it half way up to form the legs. Turn up the end of the legs to form the feet. Place a piece of spaghetti in the body to assist in holding the head in place. The arms are long ovals thinned at the top and the bottoms are curved in to form the hands. Attach the pieces with gum glue. Roll a ball for the head and flatten it slightly. Paint the face and trim it with white food color or white royal icing.

To mold a snowman by hand, roll three sizes white fondant balls. A red fondant string is used for the scarf. Roll out black fondant and cut a circle for the hat brim. Roll a ball of black fondant and flatten a little for the top of the hat.

Put the pieces together for this result.

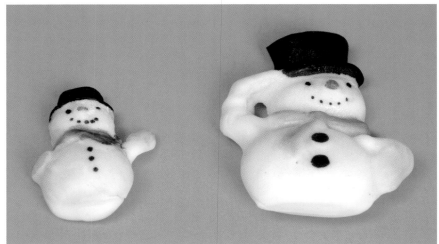

Snowmen also can be molded in candy molds and painted with food color and Vodka

The ball can be further enhanced with purchased ornaments like these.

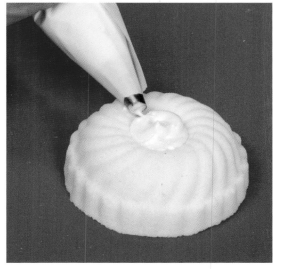

When the background of the ball is painted, pipe frosting on the top of the dried sugar base.

Place the sugar ball on top of the base and use a can to support the ball to insure that it will stay in place. Leave the support in place until the ball is thoroughly dry.

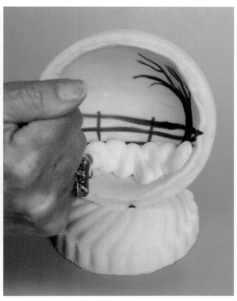

Add snow with royal icing...

... and generously sprinkle with edible glitter.

Place the tree into the ball...

... and place the snowman beside it. Pipe around the opening and add a decorative sprig of holly.

Add royal icing stars around the base where the ball sits on the base.

## *Penguin Wedding*

This adorable little couple is certain to capture the ambiance of a "cool wedding" amid the blue ice and drifting snow. The three-tier creation is baked in oval pans and frosted with blue fondant.

Various household items can be used to mold trees.

Mold with the standard sugar mixture and when it has dried about 1/4 inch deep, scrape out the inside of the tree so that there will not be as much weight. The branches of the trees were piped with either #71 or #16 star tip decorator.

As noted earlier, ice cream cones can be cut and stacked to make different heights of trees. On a layer cake like this, however, there is not enough room for a whole ice cream cone. Instead, you can roll very tight parchment paper cones. Even if the shape is not exactly what you want, they will be covered with green royal icing.

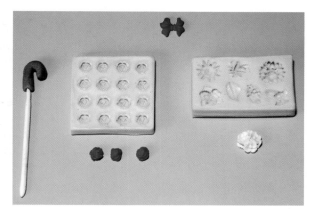

Molds are used for the penguin bride's bouquet and head piece. The cane for the groom is molded free hand. Cut a piece of tulle 3 inches by 4 inches and gather one end of the tulle with a needle and thread. Add a small amount of black royal icing to the bride's head and place the small white flower cluster on top. Add her bouquet and the grooms cane before adding the wings.

You can use paper or parchment cones rolled to the size you prefer. Plastic wine glasses can be used but do not use glass as the sugar will stick to it. For the large tree a cone was made from mylar plastic.

Roll out a thin piece of black fondant.

Mold scrap pieces of fondant into cone shapes for the base of the penguin bodies. Insert a straw in their centers. For larger forms the core needs to dry some so it will hold its shape when the excess fondant is applied.

Add a little water to the back of the black fondant and wrap it around the body base.

Use scissors to cut off the excess fondant and smooth the edges.

Form all of the penguin pieces as pictured. The head is molded over a small sucker. Cut some excess from the sucker stick if needed. Roll two balls for the feet. Flatten one end and mark the toes. Cut a circle for the brim of the hat, roll a ball and flatten it for the top of the hat. Two small ovals are shaped for the eyes, with black fondant pearls for the pupils. A small cone shape is formed for the beak. Cut out a circle and roll it into a long oval for the wings.

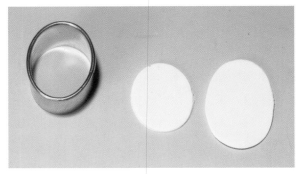

Cut two ovals with an oval cutter for the white "bibs" of the penguins. Roll one a little longer for the groom. Place the ovals on the front of the penguins. Add the head and other features.

Plastic bells are great to mold sugar bells. Use them to mold sugar bells for Christmas and wedding cakes.

Frost and stack the cake tiers. Position the trees and penguins then add royal icing snow, drifting it up on the sides with a spoon.

Generously sprinkle edible glitter over the cake while the royal icing is still wet.

# Baby Shower Sweets

Babies come at every season, filling the world with a sweetness all their own! These sweet designs will add to the celebration of these very special moments.

## *Baby Cake*

The egg is a symbol of birth, so what could be more appropriate for a baby shower than a frilly bassinet created from a molded sugar egg? The blanket can be any color to match the shower theme. With the tiny baby nestled under the covers, it is sure to delight the new mother as well as the shower guests and will be an ornament that mom can save as a keepsake.

The baby design cake is a two-layer, oval cake with a sugar molded bassinet, molded fondant bear and lamb, and fondant formed letters and covered board. The fondant is textured with an impression mat. (If you do not have this type of mat, you can texture it with a square from the type of plastic sheets that cover florescent lights, which is what was used for the design on this cake).

The decorative pieces can be made days in advance of decorating the actual cake. Mold the baby bassinet with moist sugar in a two-piece egg mold. This one was molded in a plastic cut glass egg candy mold, but the variety of available eggs is extensive.

The bottom of the egg is used for the bed portion of the bassinet. After the sugar has dried several hours, scrape only 1/3 inch out of the bed portion. The bottom half will need to dry a couple of days. You may wish to make several bassinets at a time due to the drying time between steps.

The hood of the bassinet is molded in the top half of the mold. Pack with moist sugar. Turn out and use a taut thread to cut off a portion to form the hood. It is a little less than half of the mold. Be sure to cover the cut edge with moist towels to prevent it from drying too fast. Mold a base in a plaque mold or an appropriate shape dish and allow it to dry.

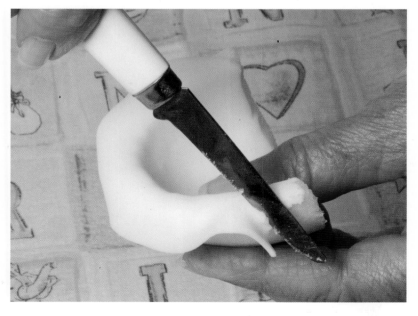

When the pieces are dry and scooped out, a fondant lining can be added to the interior. For the hood, roll a thin layer of fondant, moisten, place it inside the top and press firmly with your fingertips. Dip your fingers in cornstarch if necessary to avoid sticking.

Trim the excess.

To line the bed area, cut a fondant oval that is slightly larger than the shape of the egg. Moisten the fondant with a light spray of water and press the fondant into the cavity of the bed. Allow a small amount to stick up in the back where it will connect with the hood.

Add royal icing to the edge of the hood and attach to the base of the bassinet.

To form a baby blanket, dust an impression mat lightly with cornstarch. Roll the fondant very thin and use the impression mat to texture the fondant. Press firmly with your hands or roll over the mat with a rolling pin to press the design into the fondant.

Remove impression mat from blanket and use an oval cutter to cut the blanket shape.

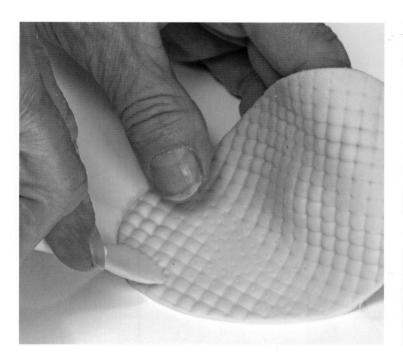

Thin the edge of the blanket and texture with a gum paste modeling tool. Cut a portion from the top edge of the blanket.

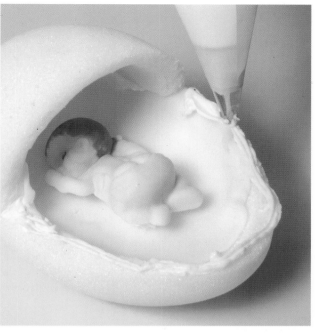

Add royal icing inside the bed and place a dried baby into it. Apply a small line of royal icing around the edge of the bassinet to hold it in place...

...and arrange the blanket over the baby.

## Making a Sleeping Baby

To create a hand-molded baby, start with an oval shape of flesh colored fondant for the body that is more narrow at the head end. Make an indentation with a small ball tool to form the area where the legs will attach.

The head is a ball shape. Use a ball tool to make a small indention in the bottom of the head and attach to the narrow end of the body. Use the small end of a #6 or #7 piping tip to make a curved mark for a sleepy eye. Form a tiny ball for the nose and a tiny oval for the ears. After the ear is added to the head, use a small round tool to hollow out the ear.

To form an arm, use a long oval shape which is pinched in two places to form the elbow and the wrist. Flatten the small end for the hand. Cut a "V" shape with small scissors to form the thumb. Use a thin knife to mark the fingers.

The leg is formed by rolling a long oval with the shape similar to a question mark. Make a slight indention in the body and attach the arm and leg with a little water or gum glue.

The baby is lying on its side so you will only need one arm, one leg and one ear.

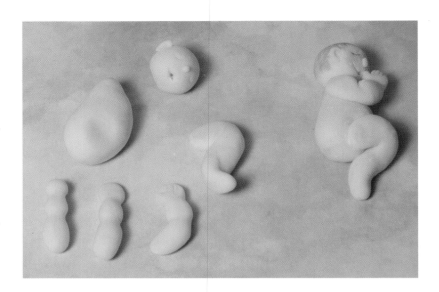

## Making a Baby Lamb

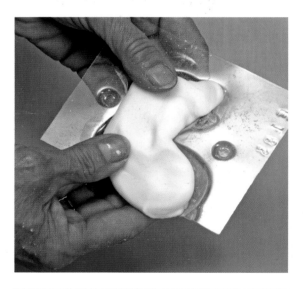

Dust a three-dimensional mold with cornstarch and press the fondant into the front half. Some 3-D candy molds come with a solid bottom and some are open. If you have the choice, choose one that has a solid bottom.

Molded lamb

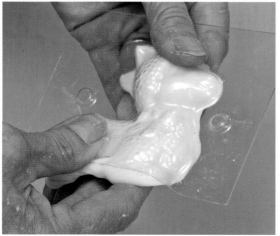

Turn the mold over to be sure that the fondant does not overflow the edge of the shape of the lamb. Use a small knife to cut off any excess fondant. The little bow is colored with food color and alcohol. The lamb's face and ears are painted with powdered colors. The eyes, nose and mouth are applied with a food safe pen.

## Making Bears: Two Methods

The first method for molding the bear starts by molding a brown, pear-shaped piece. Shape the smaller portion to form the snout and pinch the ears. The legs are formed by rolling a small oval shape slightly curved and flattened at the top edge for connection. The eyes, nose and paw prints are added with a food safe pen.

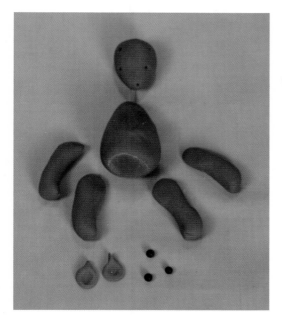

A second method to form bears starts with forming a small cone shape. With your fingers, make small indentations at the top and the bottom to place the arms and legs. Insert a small piece of spaghetti into the top of the cone. To form the head, roll a ball in the palm of your hand and shape one side to a slight point to form a snout. Make indentions into the head for eyes with a skewer or toothpick. Moisten the eye sockets and insert black fondant pearls. Form the legs by rolling long ovals that are slightly curved. Turn up the foot area. Flatten the top edge and attach with gum glue. For the ears, roll a small ball and taper one end. Use a ball tool to make indentions in the ear and let it dry. It is a good idea to make the ears in advance. Be sure to make two ears.

## Adding a Pattern to the Side of the Cake

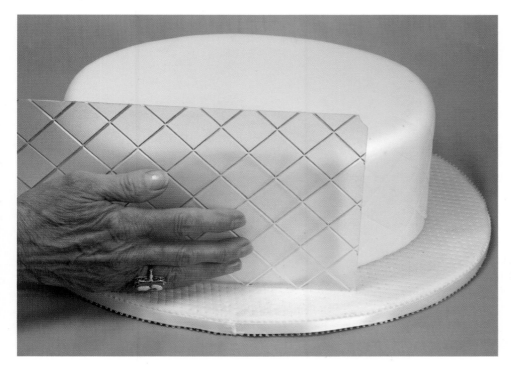

Impressing side of cake Use a diamond texture impression mat to press the design onto the side of the cake.

To complete the design arrange the bassinet, bear and lamb onto the cake and add a gum paste rose and leaves to the top of the cake. Arrange the fondant letters that are formed in advance to form the message of your choice. Dust the letters with pearl luster.

## *Petite Baby Bassinets*

Tiny bassinets can be made using the same procedure, only with petite molds.

If it looks like a football but is shaped like an egg, it is an egg mold. Some of these molds are used to hold small candies and most do not have one flat side for the base. To achieve a flat bottom, make a sanding board by gluing sandpaper to a mat board or a cake board. Sand the dried egg slightly so it will sit flat. A tiny tart pan makes a good base.

Dry all parts and assemble as described for the larger bassinet.

Silicone molds for very small babies are available through cake decorating supply shops. Mold these babies from fondant, allow them to dry then paint the hair and features.

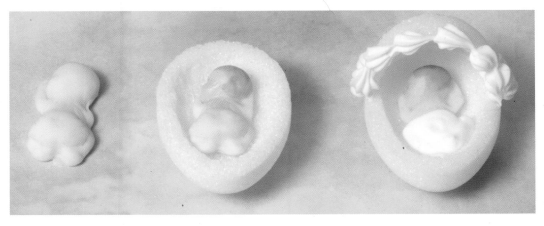

Place the baby in the bassinet and finish as with the larger figure.

For an extra special little touch for your baby shower, mold tiny baby shoes in a candy mold from moist sugar. These can be served as sugar cubes with your coffee or tea. The guests will be delighted. A second option would be to mold mints in these tiny molds. Mix 1/2 cup clear Karo syrup, 1/2 cup butter, and enough powdered sugar so that the dough is not sticky. You can flavor the candies with peppermint, spearmint, or the flavor of your choice. It is best to use oil flavoring found in the candy area of cake store or drug stores. Be careful when adding the flavoring because the oils are very strong. Roll a ball of the mixture and roll it in granulated sugar. Turn the mints out and let them dry for awhile before storing in the refrigerator or placing in a candy dish.

Molded baby bootie mints

# Receipts

## *Sugar for Molding*

1-1/2 teaspoon water
1 cup sugar
Mix the two ingredients thoroughly with your hands and keep covered.

## *Pastillage*

1 pound powdered sugar
3 Tablespoons water
2 Tablespoons lemon juice
1 envelope unflavored gelatin (1 Tablespoon)
1 heaping teaspoon glucose (do not substitute corn syrup)

## *Simple Syrup*

Mix equal parts granulated sugar and water
Boil the mixture for 3 minutes and allow to cool before using

## *Gum Glue*

1 teaspoon powdered gum Arabic
3 teaspoons water
Stir or shake in a small jar to mix. Let the mixture sit until it looses the milky
appearance and thickens.

## *Royal Icing*

3 Tablespoons meringue powder
6 Tablespoons water
1 pound powdered sugar
1/4 teaspoon cream of tartar

# Suppliers

AmeriColor
341 C. Melrose Street
Placentia, CA 92870

Marithe de Alvarado
Avenue Cuauhtemoc 950
Col. Narvarte
03020 Mexico, D.F.
011-525-523-7493

Cal-Java International
19521 Business Center Drive
Northridge, CA 91324
www.caljavaonline.com

Bakery Craft
P.O. Box 37
West Chester, OH 45071
1-800-543-1673
www.bakerycrafts.com

CK Products
310 Racquet Drive
Fort Wayne, IN 46825
219-484-2517
www.ckproducts.com

Conways Confections
Darlene Nold
12220 Shelbyville Road
Louisville, KY 40243
502-245-1010
www.conwaysconfections.com

Country Kitchen
4621 Speedway Drive
Fort Wayne, IN 46825
www.shopcountrykitchen.com

Cracker Barrel Old Country Store
www.crackerbarrel.com

Beth Parvu Sugarpaste, LLC
538 East Ewing Avenue
South Bend, IN 46613
574-233-6525
www.sugarpaste.com

PME Sugarcraft Tools
Distributed by CK Products
Fort Wayne, IN 46824
mail@ckproducts.com

Carol Webb The Cakery
2118 Meadow Place SE
Albany, OR 97321-5560
www.elegantlacemolds.com

Wilton Industries
2240 W. 75th Street
Woodbridge, IL 60571
1-888-824-9520
www.wilton.com

Sugar Craft Cake and Candy Supplies
3665 Dixie Highway
Hamilton, Ohio 45015
513-896-7089
www.sugarcraft.com

Sweet Expressions
P.O. Box 218
Abbeville, SC 29620-0218

Enjoy the Art
Share your Talent
Inspire Someone

## About the Photographer

Stringer Photography, owned by husband and wife team Sam and Elaine Stringer, is a unique, personalized studio offering the latest in technology as well as old time service. The Stringers have built a successful business by building strong relationships between themselves and their customers. They are members of the Greater Louisville Professional Photographers Association, Kentucky Professional Photographers Association, Wedding and Portrait Photographers International, Greater Louisville Better Business Bureau, and the Professional Photographers of America.

The Stringers completed the photographic work for Geraldine's last two books, *Cake of Love* and *Cakes for All Occasions.* They are also the photographers for her segments of "Kids in the Kitchen" for *Mail Box News.* Currently, Sam and Elaine are the official photographers for The International Cake Exploration Societé (I.C.E.S.). Without their patience, encouragement, perseverance, and artistic eye, this project could not have been completed. Our special thanks go out to these great friends and talented artists. They can be contacted at 502-222-8122 or stringerphoto@bellsouth.net .

Barbara Green, left, & Geraldine Kidwell

Barbara Green, from Winchester, Kentucky, is a cake artist and television demonstrator who loves to share the secrets of her success in sugar molding and figure piping. Thirty years experience as a cake decorating instructor, as well as her background as a cake supply shop owner and wedding cake designer, shine through in her work. She is a talented artist who excels in numerous artistic crafts, including hand painting tote bags and aprons, that delight the cake decorating world. Barbara has previously demonstrated her sugar molding secrets on a how-to DVD that would be an asset to every decorator, both amateur and professional.

Geraldine Kidwell, from Milton, Kentucky, has also been active in the cake art world for nearly thirty years. She is a charter member, past president, and Hall of Fame member of The International Cake Exploration Societé. She has four previous books including *Gum Paste Figures & Fashion*, *Cakes of Love*, *Cakes for all Occasions*, and *A Year of Cup Cakes*.